How
to
Manage
Management

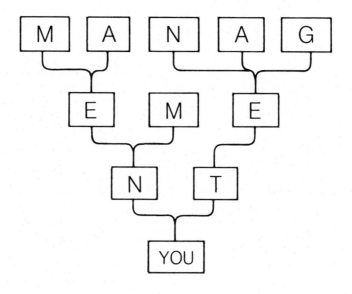

How
to
Manage
Management

by

WILLIAM E. PERRY

THE VANGUARD PRESS

NEW YORK

*This book is dedicated
to the subordinates of the world,
whose lives can be brightened by
the practice of these time-tested theories.
They really work.
Using them will put the "fun" back
into your job
as you again become the master of
your own destiny.*

Acknowledgments

We grow up believing in myths, and when one is destroyed we lose some of the joy and richness of life. When my father explained his frustrations at management's unwillingness to accept new ideas, I fought that as strongly as not believing in the tooth fairy. Now I know my father was right about management. But if I lose any more teeth, I'll still put them under my pillow.

This book is my story, this is my song. If the tune sounds familiar, it's because we all dance to the same music played by management. I learned the theories in this book in different ways. Some were painfully inflicted, others were taught by lovers of the organization. Sometimes I laughed about situations, other times I cried. Some who taught me dreamed about rising in their organization and reaping its rewards. But most dreamed of climbing over its walls to freedom.

The joy and inspiration for this labor of love came from many dear friends.

My deepest gratitude goes to Don Anders who put so much of himself into this book, with his ideas, his words—and he is a believer.

Special thanks go to those who helped me see organizations the way they really are. These great people showed me that there's humor in all situations if you look for it:

Art Engert, Laurie McConnell, Jim Maurer, Pete

ACKNOWLEDGMENTS

Warner, Ken Donoghue, Ray Woody, Phyliss Parker, Bill & Barbara Mair, Keagle Davis, Martha Platt, and Carol Gross.

For every bit of darkness there's a little bit of light, and my light during the dark days was my wife Cindy. She was there when a frustrating staff meeting cost me a fender and bumper, she was there when my mental health was in jeopardy, and she was there encouraging me when the paper for this story was blank. Thank you, Cindy, for being there.

Contents

The Sorry State of Affairs of Managers   1

The Cast of Characters   9

How Management Can Be Managed
   (or, Perry's Principles of Management)   19

The Practice of Managing Management   27

GROUP
1

Theories to Control the Use of Management's
Money—33
Creeping Commitment—35
Double-Cut—43
Man on the Moon—49
Rathole—53
Fudge Factor—59

GROUP
2

Theories Designed to Make Management Consider
You Worthy of Promotion—65
Both Ends of the Clock—67
Blue Mold—73
Glass House—77
Personal Dow-Jones—83

CONTENTS

Seventy-thirty—89
Turn the Herd—93
Alibi File—99
Company Photograph—105
Calendar—111
Paper Avalanche—117
Walking Encyclopedia—123

GROUP
3

Theories Designed to Make Management Do It
Your Way—127
Trial Balloon—129
Gimme—135
Atom Bomb—141
Hammer—145
Negative-Positive—151
Pocket Veto—157
Show and Tell—163
Camel—173

GROUP
4

Theories for Avoiding Management's Quicksand
for Subordinates—181
Top Grape—183
We Gotcha—191
Don't Wish for a New King—197
Gofor—203

CONTENTS

"Oh, by the Way"—209
Harem—215
Fossilization—221
Spinning Plate—227
You're Right, Ivan—231

GROUP
5

Theories to Make Life at Work Easier for Yourself
in Spite of Management—237

Potted Plant—239
Double Desk—245
Deep Six Theory—249
Inside the Gate—255
Mental Health—259
Oh, God—263
Houdini—267

The Lesson (or, If Someone Doesn't Point the Ship
in the Right Direction, It Will Crash)—273

The Sorry State
of Affairs of
Managers

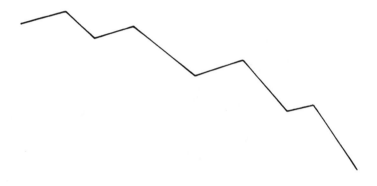

Once upon a time, there was an average organization called The Average Retail Store (TARS). Its president, I. M. Average, enjoyed average success in running the business. I.M.'s income was average, too. His employees worked an average length of time, and his customers purchased an average amount of merchandise, so the turnover and the cash flow were average. President Average was living a pretty good life, relaxing in his average executive suite and watching his average sales charts show average increases.

Then one day President Average learned that Big Retail Outlets was planning to open a huge outlet right next to his store. Darkness settled over his executive suite. The darkness thickened and despair set in when I.M. heard that, since Big Outlets wanted to corner the market, it was going to open a second outlet on the other side of The Average Retail Store. President Average ranted and raved. He berated his employees. He paced the floor. He even stopped sleeping nights. The only thing President Average didn't do was provide a plan to keep TARS viable and profitable. The day for the grand opening of Big Outlets' two new stores was drawing close. The buildings were completed and stocked with the latest merchandise. Got the picture? Here is The Average Retail Store squeezed right in between two huge retail outlets.

Since President Average had no plan, he called all his subordinates in and told them, "Get busy!" Before dawn on the day of the grand opening of the two huge outlets, a truck pulled up to the little store in the middle. Four men got out ladders, tools, and a big billboard. With great difficulty they attached the huge sign to a hoist, raised it up above the doors of The Average Retail Store, and fastened it to the wall.

One of the president's subordinates ordered the men to remove the covering from the sign. On it were two words: MAIN ENTRANCE.

Inside, the manager had decorated the store for a gala sale. Each department head had marked down his merchandise enough to compete with Big Outlets and still make a profit. All the salespeople were told that this was their chance to save their jobs and earn a bonus. So what do you think happened?

When Big Outlets opened their doors, The Average Retail Store did too. The customers started shopping in TARS and found fair prices, good merchandise, and helpful salespeople who cared about them. Not only did The Average Retail Store have its best sales day ever; sales broke records for the next forty weeks. The employees made more money, and everybody lived happily ever after.

What about President I. M. Average? When he saw how well things went, he decided he could spend more time in Miami. The more time he spent in Miami, the better things went . . . so he spent more time in Miami. The moral? If the average manager gets desperate enough, he will let the people who know how (his subordinates) run the business. Unfortunately, most subordinates have to run the business with the added problem of keeping the boss from interfering. This book is designed to help you—the subordinate—manage management until they decide to spend more time in Miami.

If you have studied traditional management theory, you know that it provides the manager with guidance and direction on motivating, influencing, and directing subordinates. However, these theories have one great failing. They fail to recognize how much subordinates affect the overall functioning of the organization. President I. M. Average is typical of the person at the top. All too often, the manager or president is a captain standing at the helm of a rudderless ship traversing the high seas under full sail. Even if the tiller he so adroitly moves this way and that were attached to a rudder, it wouldn't help. His perception of what is happening and what lies ahead has little effect on the course of the ship. In fact, most captains of industry prefer to take down the sails and just drift. Perhaps that's where the expression "Don't rock the boat" got started.

The fact is that subordinates are running most organizations while their managers strive mightily to avoid decisions and maintain the status quo. It's high time that the subordinates learned how to manage their managers by objective, not by chance. For once the subordinate gets his rudder in the water, he can guide the ship through stormy seas to a safe harbor—even with the "captain" at the helm.

Profile of a Modern Manager

Over the past twenty-five years I have been a student of management. During that time personal observation and the consensus of literally hundreds of subordinates have provided this profile of the typical manager:

Species: Homo sapiens
Sex: Male
Age: 53.6
Weight: 182 pounds
Height: 5' 11"
Married an average of 1.4 times
Family of 2.4 children (.4 takes after Daddy)
Brown hair (slightly graying at the temples)
Lives in a home costing $63,800

Education: 4.6 years of college (3.2 business adminis-
tration, 1.4 technical)
Reading habits: Avid subscriber to *Wall Street Journal,*
Forbes, and *Playboy*
A member of 1.3 clubs (of which .4 is a country club)
A regular church attender who has served in some po-
sition of responsibility
Travels an average of 15.8 nights per year (average trip
is between 100 and 200 miles from home)

So there's the picture. The modern manager looks and
acts much as we would expect. He is the all-American boy, the
college graduate, the homeowner, the family man, a pillar of
the community, a little above average height, every bit the
manager image. Now let's look closer. After all, only haber-
dashers believe that clothes make the man. What are the manager's attitudes?

Yes. We must find out how our typical manager thinks
and feels. Why? How else can we understand some of the
crazy things he does? So let's look into the attitudes of the average manager; they should be revealing:

72.6% are happy (and not sure why).
81.2% feel insecure in their present position (the Peter
Principle syndrome).
43.6% feel they have reached the highest position they
will ever hold in the organization.
57.8% doubt their ability to perform well in their present position.

93% care much more about their company than about
their subordinates.

89% feel subordinates do not appreciate what managers do for them.

63% feel they are underpaid for what they do.

94.7% do not understand the technical skills required
of the subordinates who report to them.

Only 14% feel they will retire before technological ad-
vances make them obsolete.

78% prefer subordinates with less education than they
have.

63% prefer to have their subordinates deal with their
secretaries rather than with themselves directly.

71% withhold negative comments about their subordinates because they dread arguments with them.

54% feel they are less free now than in their previous
position.

81% feel they have no one to confide in, so they keep
their frustrations and personal feelings to
themselves.

87% feel there is much more pressure in their current
position than in the last one.

38% dread a promotion.

Now, that is not a pretty picture. Behind the image we
find the real man—the modern manager. Our all-American
boy is somewhat insecure, a little behind the times technically,
and feels threatened by both his subordinates and his boss.
Perhaps he is not to blame. Perhaps society has required too

much of him. That is a question for further study. We are not attempting to resolve that issue here. What we *are* doing is telling you how to maneuver your manager into a position where you can guide the ship of industry or business in the right direction. We all know the managers need help despite their outward protestations of competence. You can and should provide the needed assistance. This book will show you how.

The Cast
of
Characters

Norman New's boyhood dream has come true. Easy Sales Corporation, one of the Lucky 500, has hired him. Norman has just graduated from Cape Able College. Norm was third in his class, played on the football team, and served as sergeant-at-arms on the student government. He had everything going for him. True to form, Norman married his childhood sweetheart, Tru Bleu. It's July 1 and Norman is reporting to the personnel department of Easy Sales Corp.

To make a good first impression, Norman arrives fifteen minutes before starting time. Alone in the waiting room, Norm cannot see the mournful masses of Easy Sales Corp.'s personnel trudging to their appointed work stations. Of course, Norman does see the personnel department troops march in. After a cup of coffee and discussion of their weekend activities, Norman New is called into the personnel director's office. After a perfunctory greeting, Norman fills out forms, signs authorizations for taxes, survivors' rights, and several other rights as well as presenting to Easy Sales Corp. every certificate earned, given, or won since birth. At last the initiation rites are completed and Norman is one of them. Congratulations, Norm!

Norman's first assignment is to meet the "guys." So he takes the traditional walk from personnel to his department, accompanied by Wendy Watch, a secretary, who introduces him around. Norm notices that Wendy is young and sweet. She does what she is told, no more. He will also learn later that she is never late for work, for a rest break, going to lunch, returning from lunch, or going home. Wendy is at ease with the "guys" and loves to hear about their personal problems. Norm will learn never to ask Wendy to do anything five minutes before quitting time, for her once sweet look turns sour enough to curdle your coffee.

First of all, Norm meets Mary Mouth. She holds a key position in the organization. Mary is fifty-two years old and plump, and wears pantsuits. Mary has gained seniority; she has been with the company longer than anyone else. During this time she has been busy politicking—building up her authority by association. You always know exactly what authority Mary has because she is quick to remind you of it. Norman will quickly learn that he cannot bypass Mary Mouth if her authority extends anywhere near his activities. You remember those World War II fighter pilots who painted symbols on the sides of their planes for every enemy aircraft shot down? Mary could have all sides of her desk painted with symbols of projects, ideas, and people she has shot down over the years. Norman had better keep out of her sights.

"And this is Randy Rightman," introduces Wendy. Norman will find that Randy is the backbone of the company. Randy has been coming to work on time for thirty-two years and never leaves for home and hearth until the job of the day is done, and done right! In Randy's mind the company is next to God. The company is right, and what is good for Easy Sales Corp. is good for Randy Rightman. Randy's greeting to Norman is cordial but brief. You see, Randy has to get back to work. Norm won't find Randy hanging around the water cooler or cafeteria joking with the others. He is all business. True, you get the idea he is some kind of martyr, but somebody has to do the work and Randy is that somebody. Norman will see Randy in and out of the boss's office often. What he may not find out is that Randy is loath to do anything without first checking with the boss. What the boss wants, Randy wants. During his introduction tour, Norman meets two others very similar to Randy. They are Will Workman and Swann Songue, thirty-year men.

"Norman New, meet Sam Smoothwater," coos Wendy. "Hi, Norm," says Sam. "Did you hear the one about the . . ." This is the first in a never-ending series of stories and one-liners Norman will hear from Sam. Quick-witted and friendly, Sam is a fun guy to have coffee or lunch with. Sam is always in a good mood, and everybody seems to like him. He's pretty successful too. Seems to know his way around.

"Here comes Penny Push," Wendy half whispers. Norman notes some apprehension in Wendy's voice. Norman smiles. "Glad to meet you, Penny," he says. He doesn't know yet that Penny will consider him a competitor. She is ambitious and not too particular about what she has to do to get promoted. There's one thing about it, Penny will do whatever the company wants her to do and do it well. She will take long assignments out of town with nary a complaint. Penny also takes work home and works nights and weekends—especially if the boss is there to see her. Penny has been known to pirate the work or ideas of others and claim them as her own.

Next, Norman meets Phil Pockets. Phil is the kind of guy who can watch a shell game at a carnival and tell you which shell the pea is under. If you have a problem, Phil has the solution. His outstanding talent is as a promoter extraordinaire. Phil is always proposing projects and starting them up. Strangely, Phil has never personally completed a project in seventeen years. Yet he gets most of the credit for completed projects. If the project fails, it's because the implementation team could not meet Phil's demanding specifications. The old soft shoe may have died with vaudeville, but Phil Pockets is keeping it alive in the corporation. Put Phil in front of management and he outperforms everyone else with his fancy footwork—a dazzling display of facts, figures, and trivia. And Phil is the only one who knows which is which.

"Ima Stickler's office is next," Wendy confides to Norm. "She is the one to see if you have questions on policy, procedure, and company tradition. Ima can recite the entire corporation charter, word for word." Norman greets Ima, and before he leaves he learns the latest policies that have been approved but not yet published. Norman believes Wendy. He will be visiting Ima from time to time, he can see that already. Norman may not find all his visits as pleasant as this first one. He'll find that Ima Stickler knows the book, lives by the book, and loves the book.

"Oh!" gasps Wendy. "What's wrong? Can I help you?" asks a startled Norman. "No, no—it's nothing," Wendy insists, visibly shaken. "Hello, Wendy," slides off the tongue of the sharp-looking young man approaching. "Oh, hello, Denny," Wendy replies. "This is Norman New." "Helll-ooo, Norman," says Denny in a resounding voice over a crushing handshake. Norman thinks he has met Denny somewhere, he seems so familiar.

You have, Norm. Everybody knows Denny Dart. He's the guy who copied off your test paper in school and you got zero for telling him to knock it off. He's the same guy who erased your name on the homework you had done and put his on it. He's the very same one who handed you the cigarettes in the restroom just as the principal walked in. Sure you know him. Denny still uses the same tricks at Easy Sales Corp. If he works on a job with someone, he'll call it a 90/10 project. He'll tell the boss he did 90 percent of the work and you did 10 percent. Of course it's the other way around. If Denny just walks through your office, he'll give your supervisor the impression he did part or all of your work that day. To your face, Denny will tell you you're a great guy, a fabulous worker, the backbone of the company, and his best friend. He will convince you how you and he need to work together to prove to management that the two of you are doing a great job. What he wants you to do is say something good about him. But when he is alone with your boss, Denny can't even remember your name.

Okay, Norman New, you have met the Indians. Let's move up another floor to meet the assistant chiefs. Wendy says, "We'll have to be more brief up here. These are our middle-level managers and they're pretty busy people." Norman will find this true today. But if he proves himself after being here awhile, the assistant chiefs will have time to talk.

"Ken Census, this is Norman New," says Wendy. Turning to Norman, she says, "You'll enjoy working with Ken. If you have any problems, he'll be glad to help." "Right," Ken says, and greets Norman with a genuine friendliness and warmth that is the first breath of fresh air since he met Sam Smoothwater. As time goes on, Norman will find Ken Census to be the kind of manager people do like to work for. Ken has some crazy ideas about management. He praises people for what they do well, and when they do badly, he understands their problems and helps them to do better next time. It's even rumored that Ken evaluates his people on what they do rather than on whether they arrive on time in the morning. Some have said Ken even allows his subordinates to disagree with him and takes their advice. Unfortunately, there aren't very many Kens in Easy Sales Corp., or anywhere else, for that matter.

Tom Tough is the man in the next office. Tom's terse greeting is typical of him. The last time Tom said anything nice was when his mother gave him a new bike on his seventh birthday. Tom is sure his subordinates are lazy and only work when being watched. When Tom leaves the office, he gives everybody a lecture on how the mice shouldn't play when the cat's away. He also "knows" a couple of other things: first, people only work for money and, second, anyone who takes sick leave is just goofing off. Norman doesn't know it now, but he'll learn to dislike Tom, and it won't take long.

In a small office at the end of the corridor, Norman finds Dee Endd. Dee retired at twenty-seven. Not from Easy Sales Corp. Just from work. She is now forty-seven and awaiting her official retirement. The last decision she made was almost ten years ago. Some say that decision was not to make other decisions. Dee Endd has a great system worked out to keep busy all day. She calls meetings. The amazing thing is how anyone can hold so many meetings and accomplish so little in so much time. Never has anyone worked so hard to keep from doing anything. Dee is the living Endd.

After a superquick greeting to Dee, Wendy says, "Norman, we'll have to be very quiet now. We're on Mahogany Row." As the elevator door closes, Wendy says, "Here is where you'll find the real chiefs. This office we're coming to belongs to Harvey Harpooner, the corporate controller. He holds the purse strings."

Mr. Harpooner gives Norman his widest corporate smile, which somehow ends up looking like a cross between a crocodile and Bert Parks. On the way to the next office, which is quite some distance away, Wendy explains in hushed tones that Mr. Harpooner has the sharpest pencil in the East. He cuts up detailed reports and uses them for scratch pads. Harpooner has also been known to walk a mile and a half from the airline terminal to his hotel carrying two large suitcases and a briefcase to save taxi fare. Mr. Harpooner is the guardian of corporate assets and cherishes the position. They call him Old Double-Cut, for reasons you'll find out later. Rumor has it that Harpooner hasn't cashed his first paycheck yet.

A few other corporate chieftains greet Norman, and Wendy says, "Now I'll show you Ivan Kingman's desk. Here's his office now. Take a look." What Norman sees is impressive. Kingman's desk is massive. His furniture is the most expensive money can buy. His desk accessories cost more than most people's office furniture. "Here is a man who is an unqualified success," thinks Norman.

You're right, Norm. Ivan Kingman is the big man, top dog, chief executive officer, and oracle of Easy Sales Corp. If you can't get to be President of the United States, the next best thing is Ivan Kingman's job. Ivan's got it all. A chauffeured limousine, a company jet, a company yacht, two company apartments strategically located, and a well-stocked bar in his office.

"You'll have to meet Mr. Kingman later, Norman. He is out of town this week," Wendy says. Little does Norman know he may never meet Ivan Kingman. He is just too busy.

Kingman is president of his college alumni association, serves on four boards of directors of prestigious firms, is vice-chairman of the local community fund, is a volunteer director of the local chamber of commerce, is active in his church, sponsors a Little League softball team, and is vice-president of a major trade association. In addition to all this, Kingman has made twenty-seven speeches in twenty-seven different cities this year. (Not different speeches, however.) Oh, yes, he also attended the opening of seven new sales locations in seven different cities. And we mustn't forget the two-week seminar he attended at a major university. Yes, sir, Ivan Kingman is a busy man. Easy Sales Corp. couldn't do without him for a day!

"Well, that's it," exclaims Wendy. "What do you think of it?" "It's colossal," says Norman with a low whistle. "I don't know exactly what I expected, but whatever it was, this is bigger. Lead me to my desk. I can't wait to get started."

How Management Can Be Managed

OR

Perry's Principles of Management

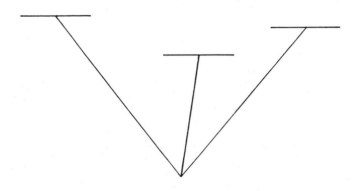

Traditionally, management is viewed as providing top–down direction, with all wisdom and guidance coming from above. Those who accept this view envision the modern manager sitting in the executive suite barking orders and confidently pushing buttons which cause his subordinates to take the proper course of action. In the real world, it's not that way at all.

Bottom–up management is typical in most organizations. What really happens is that the "manager" waits to see which way the wind is blowing from his subordinates, and then sets sail in the direction that will carry him the farthest. In bottom–up management the subordinates make all the decisions. As a result, the manager is never wrong. If things don't work out, he blames his subordinates. If they do, he takes the credit.

It's time we discussed Perry's Principles of Management. They differ greatly from the traditional principles— Perry's principles are true. They are:

(1) Management, like gravity, is a holding force with a primary function of preventing ideas from rising to acceptance.

(2) Management does not want to hear the truth.

(3) Management does not want to make decisions.

Since these principles have a tremendous impact on modern business and government, we will discuss each of them in turn.

Perry's First Principle of Management could be summed up in the statement: Management is fighting to maintain the status quo. There is good reason for this. Perhaps the most vital reason is that the manager does not understand the technical operations of those he manages. Since this is so, the manager is required to decide about things he doesn't understand. That's like driving a car and asking a blind man next to you to estimate the distance between you and the car in front of you.

The easiest way out for the manager is to make no decisions and to squelch all ideas but those for which the arguments are irrefutable. Today's managers have rewritten the old proverb "Nothing ventured, nothing gained" to say "Nothing tried, nothing lost."

Surprisingly enough, the higher the level of management, the more negative the manager becomes. For instance, a foreman will accept more recommendations than he rejects. A chief executive officer rarely accepts a suggestion. Thus, we can anticipate the status quo(tient) of a manager by knowing at which level he appears on the organization chart. The reason why top-level managers are less inclined to accept ideas than foremen is that they are so far removed from technical operations that they understand little or nothing of what they are told. Foremen at least know something about what is going on around them.

Perry's Second Principle states that managers do not want to hear bad news. This principle is not new, just true. It really harks back to Biblical times when the king's messengers would personally bring word from the battlefront. If the messenger declared good news, he was rewarded with expensive jewels and the finest gold. But woe betide the messenger who brought bad news. The disgruntled king would bellow, "Off with his head!" Centuries have passed, but have times really changed?

Today we call our kings "chief executive officers" and our messengers "subordinates." As in the past, messengers declaring good news get raises and promotions. But what about the subordinate who carries bad news to the boss? He finds himself fired—or worse, in the Cleveland branch.

What's a body to do? Obviously, you are going to do your darnedest to pass on good news to the king . . . er, the chief executive officer. We hear our corporate kings complaining, "No one will tell me the truth!" Have they forgotten that they haven't changed the rules their predecessors made up centuries ago?

Perry's Third Principle of Management is the big-business version of "Heads I win, tails you lose." Your boss, the manager on the next level up from you, will not say yes to anything unless you present enough proof to win your case before the Supreme Court. The reason is obvious; he just wants to be sure you are sure you know what you're doing. If so, he will reluctantly allow you to act "against his better judgment." This is where "Heads I win, tails you lose" comes in. If you succeed, he accepts all the accolades. If you fail, he blames you. A great spot for him, but a lousy one for you.

These three principles explain the actions of the modern manager. As you have seen, the manager not only wants things to stay as they are, he practically insists that they do. This rejection posture justifies your efforts to manage management. Since they fear new ideas, progress depends on your use of flanking maneuvers to move management in the right direction to achieve good results.

Perry's Pertinent Premises

Now that you are familiar with Perry's Principles of Management, you need to know about Perry's Pertinent Premises. They are:

(1) Your boss is no wiser than you are.

(2) Your boss has no more confidence in his abilities than you do in yours.

(3) Once becoming boss, he operates under Perry's Principles of Management.

You may find these premises hard to accept unless you have had many years of experience in the business world. However, they are true. And once you realize this, you can see the importance of subordinates like yourself. This very knowledge is power.

Think about it. Can you see the possibilities for managing management if they are mere humans like you and me? The fact is that there are many opportunities to manage management in the day-to-day operation of any organization. The primary purpose of this book is to help you to get the most out of your manager, for your good and the good of your company.

As I have pointed out, managing management requires the judicious use of flanking maneuvers. The managing-management hypothesis states that such maneuvers are engaged in every day. However, this modus operandi has yet to be recognized as a full-fledged, valid philosophy for operating organizations. Perhaps one reason is that, though widely practiced, the hypothesis has not been adequately researched or fully documented. This book should fill that vacuum.

As you observe the operation of your own organization, you have probably wondered:

Why is it that Will Workman was never promoted beyond his

current position when everyone knows he does all the work?

Why is it that every time you work with Denny Dart, he seems to get all the credit while you do all the work? Yet when Denny and you talk, he always makes you feel so important.

How can Ivan Kingman run this corporation when he is never here?

Why is it that Phil Pockets always seems to have enough money in his budget after having it reviewed by Harvey Harpooner and you don't?

The answer, is quite simple. Some subordinates understand how managers operate and use that knowledge to manipulate management to get things done. The Will Workmans and Randy Rightmans of the world are always struggling to make do with the few bones tossed to them by management. The Denny Darts and Phil Pocketses of the world are getting ahead by managing management.

This book contains the forty most successful theories on how to manage management. You'll find Denny Dart and Phil Pockets using them every day while Will Workman and Randy Rightman stumble along believing that right makes might and good triumphs over evil. They are so naïve that they think all they need to do is work hard and they will eventually be recognized and rewarded. Sorry, Randy and Will, that's not the way organizations work.

Today you can only make things happen if you understand the principles and premises upon which modern management is based. Then, if you use the field-tested, commonly practiced theories of managing management, you will at last find satisfaction and recognition, to say nothing of fame and fortune.

In the following pages these theories will be clearly stated and illustrated to help you develop strategies for personal and organizational progress. Mr. or Ms. Subordinate, the theories presented in this volume should be studied and applied to assure acceptance of your ideas and the success of your endeavors.

The Practice of Managing Management

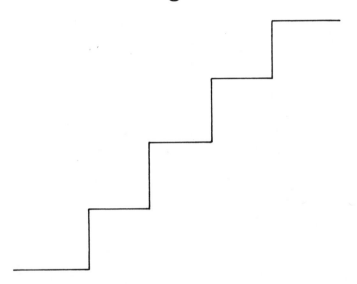

As a subordinate, you will often be placed in a position where you will be expected to accomplish something and find that your boss is the greatest obstacle to its accomplishment. Let's take a conference as an example.

Your superior, Tom Tough, tells you he wants you to plan and implement a sales conference for Easy Sales Corp. Tom explains that the conference should have class and be a memorable experience for the sales force, a real stimulus to their activities.

Then you work up a budget of, say, $10,000. You have gotten the best prices and made the arrangements exactly according to the specifications set forth by Tom. Now, when you talk to Tom about the cost, you find he is suspicious. He thinks that somehow it's a boondoggle and is reluctant to give you the money you need to put on the conference he requested. What is the solution to your dilemma? You don't know? There's a theory to help you. It's called the Double-Cut.

Here is another example. Your work is outstanding. You produce more than any other member of your department. Yet your salary increases barely meet the cost-of-living increases. Why? Perhaps you are not acquainted with the Both Ends of the Clock Theory.

You say your ideas are good and no one will listen to you. Is that your trouble, cousin? Then you had better read up on the Blue Mold Theory. Would you like to know why a project you calculate to be a disaster with a monstrous overrun is considered successful and is expected to bring in an excellent return on investment? Then you need to understand the Rathole Theory.

The forty theories in this book are field-tested and true. They are in use throughout the worlds of business and government. They may seem humorous. They may seem devious. They may seem undesirable. But, once they are illustrated, you will probably say, "That's what old What's-his-name does."

As a subordinate (or a progressive manager) you should know all these theories by heart and keep them at your fingertips. You may wish to list them on 4 x 6 cards and carry them to meetings. Then, scan the list for the theory you need or the one being used by those attending the meeting. It's a fascinating hobby—and the boss thinks you are scanning data you prepared for the meeting.

You'll find these theories in use right in your own home if you observe closely enough. Here's how to use them:

Scan the following synopsis of the forty theories. Find the phrase that explains your dilemma with management. The theory you need is in parentheses. This is your on-the-job salvation. Use it in good health, and for your own good health.

Group I — Theories to Control the Use of Management's Money

—Ask for only a little money at one time. (Creeping Commitment)

—Get the money you need to do a project right in spite of management. (Double-Cut)

—Anything can be accomplished with enough resources. (Man on the Moon)

—Out of sight, out of mind. (Rathole)

—Make what you spend always equal to what you were authorized to spend. (Fudge Factor)

Group II — Theories Designed to Make Management Consider You Worthy of Promotion.

—How to get ahead through the judicious use of twelve minutes a day. (Both Ends of the Clock)

—Know when your ideas will be accepted by management. (Blue Mold)

—Understand why management cannot do things. (Glass House)

—Time accomplishment to your personal advantage. (Personal Dow-Jones)

—Never run out of work, or your boss will give you an assignment at the bottom of the pile. (Seventy-thirty)

—Good can come out of evil if you use it properly. (Turn the Herd)

—To prove your innocence in a situation, you need evidence. (Alibi File)

—You are judged by the company you keep. (Company Photograph)

—Backdate documents to your advantage. (Calendar)

—Use a flurry of paper work to overcome concern. (Paper Avalanche)

—Use facts, both supported and unsupported, to help your cause. (Walking Encyclopedia)

Group III — Theories Designed to Make Management Do It Your Way

—Know which way to go, or what to ask for, before you do it, and be assured you're right. (Trial Balloon)

—Give the boss the needed flaw to find. (Gimme)

—Sometimes you have to hit management over the head with a two-by-four to get attention. (Atom Bomb)

—If you give a kid a hammer, the kid will find that everything needs pounding. (Hammer)

—Often you can get what you want by asking for the opposite. (Negative-Positive)

—Let the boss say no without saying no. (Pocket Veto)

—Time spent in meetings can be productive. (Show and Tell)

—Committees can build horses instead of camels. (Camel)

Group IV — Theories for Avoiding Management's Quicksand for Subordinates

—Make use of the organization's grapevine. (Top Grape)

—Don't get caught in the organization's benefits trap. (We Gotcha)

—Learn to coexist with the existing boss; a new one will probably be worse. (Don't Wish for a New King)

—Use errand-running to your own advantage. (Gofor)

—Throw the boss off guard before you get zapped. ("Oh, by the Way . . . ")

—Don't fool with the boss's collection of beauties. (Harem)

—Beware of those whose brains have turned to rock. (Fossilization)

—Don't say you can when you can't. (Spinning Plate)

—Know how to answer your boss's questions with the right answers. (You're Right, Ivan)

Group V — Theories to Make Life at Work Easier for Yourself in Spite of Management

—Get all the status symbols you're entitled to get. (Potted Plant)

—If you have two work stations, you only have to be at one or the other, or somewhere in between. (Double Desk)

—Don't do the job you don't have to do. (Deep Six)

—Never get sick or hurt off the company premises. (Inside the Gate)

—Use the company benefit programs to give you a better outlook on life. (Mental Health)

—You can mix business and religion if you do it the right way. (Oh, God)

—Never be on a ship when it sinks. (Houdini)

GROUP
1

Theories
to Control the Use
of Management's
Money

CREEPING COMMITMENT THEORY

Theory in brief:
Little decisions get the job done
When the boss won't make the biggest one.

The Creeping Commitment Theory can be voluntary or involuntary. If you know the theory, you can make it work *for* you. If you don't, watch those little decisions. They can lead to a big decision you didn't want to make. Here's an example. Henry Householder and his family were planning a cross-country vacation for next year. The whole family was looking forward to it, including Henry's wife, Henrietta. However, she also wanted the living room redone. She was putting off the redecoration because all the family's spare cash was being stashed away for the big vacation.

"Still," thought Henrietta, "we *could* afford to replace

that threadbare velvet chair we rescued from the Goodwill store years ago. Besides, Seers Robot & Co. has that darling yellow chair on sale for just $119." Henrietta counted her cash and was relieved to find that they could, indeed, afford the yellow chair. It was delivered on Friday afternoon, and it looked just great in the living room.

That night Henrietta noticed that the yellow chair didn't go too well with the flowered purple wallpaper. The next day she let her fingers do the walking through the yellow pages and they found a company that would steam off the old wallpaper for just $68. The Seers Robot catalog offered her a gallon of paint for only $9 on special. Henrietta decided that another $77 wouldn't cramp the family's vacation budget, so she forged ahead. The paint looked nice too, and the yellow chair gave just the right emphasis to the beige walls.

What was the name of that theory? Oh, yes, Creeping Commitment. By now, the total investment was $196. Not really a great deal of money. But on Sunday night when her guests left, Henrietta noticed those purple drapes. They just didn't go well with the beige walls. "Well," rationalized Henrietta, "I've gone this far, I had better get those drapes. If I don't get them now, the January sale will be over and they'll cost me twice as much." Back to Seers Robot.

No one can deny that those loose-weave drapes looked great with the beige walls and the yellow chair. In February, Henrietta saved a bundle during the carpet sale. In March, she got a 20 percent reduction on new lighting fixtures. The April furniture specials were irresistible, and Henrietta added a sofa and end table to that gorgeous living room. May saw Henrietta hanging the paintings and arranging the accessories that added the finishing touches to a living room that a Rockefeller would be proud of.

By June, Henrietta had spent $2,684 to redo the living room. The family was to begin its vacation in July. Henrietta just couldn't believe it. "All I did," she thought, "was replace that ratty old chair." No, Henrietta, you are a victim of the Creeping Commitment Theory. Needless to say, the family did not take their cross-country vacation. They could hardly afford to cross the street.

Yes, it all started with a little decision. Then another and another, until the big decision was made. Henrietta would never have committed $2,684 at one time to her living room. But little decisions are easy to make.

You've done the same thing at the swimming pool in June. The hardy ones make the big decision and jump in. But you? You say, "Not me. I'm not stupid." Your friends splash around happily, urging you on. *"Weelll,* I'll see how cold it really is," you say, sticking your big toe in the water. Pretty soon, through a series of little commitments, you are up to your waist in ice water. It isn't long before you are shivering with your freezing friends, who are laughing *at* you, not *with* you.

Even having children is a creeping commitment. If you knew that your next child would cost $225,000 over a lifetime, you might approach sex more cautiously. It's the unknown, the uncounted, the unforeseen, that aid us to make small decisions so quickly. Why is it we make a creeping commitment of $99.50 as the down payment on a car, never thinking about

37

the total of $6,245 we are really spending? Because little decisions are easy to make, that's why.

Now, how can you use the Creeping Commitment Theory to advantage in business? You want your boss to make a major decision, and you say he won't make it? Maybe not, but try him on a small decision—you'll be amazed and pleased how easily he will commit himself.

But let's talk about the three phases of the Creeping Commitment Theory. The only prerequisite for Phase 1 is that your boss recognize a problem exists. You must present it, but in doing so you must carefully avoid presenting the solution. Once management recognizes the problem, all that Phase 1 requires is a commitment to study it so you can present its scope and implications to management.

Phase 2 calls for you to present your findings along with a solution to the problem. During development of the solution, management moves slowly through the stages of ever-increasing commitment to it.

Phase 3 is the implementation of the solution. This can be done in bits and pieces, as Henrietta Householder found out, or, if the commitment has crept far enough during the presentation, full-scale implementation may occur on the spot. Let's see how Ken Census uses the Creeping Commitment Theory at Easy Sales Corp.

Ken is convinced it would save the company many person-hours and improve employee morale if Easy Sales Corp. had a lunch/recreation room on the premises. Ken also knows that the last thing Harvey Harpooner gave to the employees was free-pulling toilet paper dispensers in the restrooms, and he's never been happy about that. Nevertheless, Ken is willing to go to bat for the lunchroom. He approaches Harvey.

Watch Phase 1 in action.

"Harvey," Ken says, "as you know, many of our employees are going home for lunch and getting back late. Some others are eating lunch at their desks. This is causing noxious odors throughout our professional offices and some peanut butter stains on the desks." Harvey, as the controller, is well aware of this. He has often thought about those costly stains and the lost working time.

"Harvey," Ken continues, "why don't I spend a little time reviewing the lunch policy?" "Can't hurt," thinks Harvey. So he agrees and makes commitment number one. Phase 1 is well under way and the commitment has started to creep.

Of course, Ken has already studied the problem, but he waits two weeks before talking to Harpooner again, so Harpooner will not feel he has slighted the assignment. "Here's the problem, Harvey," says Ken. "Since employees sit at their desks or go home to eat, we can't control when lunch starts and stops." That agrees with Harpooner's assessment of the situation. So he asks Ken, "Have you come up with a solution?" "I'm not quite sure. I need a little more time to study it," says Ken. Harvey agrees, and another commitment is made.

Now we're into Phase 2. The Phase 2 study results in an elaborate report showing that the obvious solution is a special room in which the employees can eat lunch under controlled conditions. "Go to it!" says Harvey, thinking,

"Now I'll be sure to get them all back to their unstained desks within the appointed time."

Phase 3—implementation—is inevitable since the commitment has crept to the point of no return. Ken cleans out part of the stockroom and puts in a lunch table. Once the employees start using the provisional room, Ken gets a commitment for the construction of a special lunchroom, later an outside recreational area, still later an inside recreational area for inclement weather, and so on. Harvey will never know that his agreement to study the lunch policy resulted in an investment of $137,580 on something he never wanted in the first place.

Ken has done the company a real favor. They haven't had a strike in years. The employees are happy. And even though they take longer for lunch than ever, production and profits are up. Harvey Harpooner doesn't know why; he just knows Ivan Kingman is happy and that's all that matters.

The Creeping Commitment Theory works because big decisions are hard to make and very painful for most managers. It takes a creative subordinate to get a manager to make that first commitment that creeps up on the big decision.

Use this theory to help your management avoid big, painful decisions. You'll make life easier for both of you and help your company at the same time.

The moral:
Creeping commitments are easy to take
It's big decisions the boss can't make.

DOUBLE-CUT THEORY

OR

How to Get What You Need in Spite of Management

Theory in brief:
Your manager's boss expects him to cut costs in
half, so ask for twice as much as you will need.

The Double-Cut Theory has been standard procedure in the home and business since time immemorial. When you were a child (subordinate), you asked for four dollars a week and management (your parents) gave you two. When you asked to stay out until midnight, you got to stay out until ten.

Then you got out of school and went to work. It's still the same. You ask for different things from different managers, but the double cut does you in. You request $500 to attend a vital seminar. Your proposal is halved and you are told to find a seminar that is closer to headquarters, takes less time, and so forth. Your department budgets are cut, your orders for supplies are cut, and your personnel are cut. The only thing that is never cut is the number and scope of the tasks you are asked to perform.

It's time you learned to manage management with the Double-Cut Theory. It *can* work to your advantage. First, you have to ask yourself a question: "Why is it that the world seems to be divided into the haves and the have-nots?" The proper understanding and use of the Double-Cut Theory explains this difference.

The have-nots don't understand or use the theory. The haves do. The have-nots ask only for what they need and get half of that. The haves ask for twice what they need and end up getting half, which is exactly what they wanted in the first place.

Here's an example. It's all too typical, as you'll soon discern.

Two years ago Harvey Harpooner asked Will Workman to put on a conference for the regional salesmen. Since this was a kickoff for an important sales campaign, it was necessary to put on an excellent conference. Will picked out a place to hold the conference, negotiated a rock-bottom price, and figured out his budget to the last penny.

Harvey Harpooner reviewed the budget and as a competent manager was determined to cut the "fat" out of it. Ostensibly, this was to be sure Will got fair value for company funds. When Will received the budget back, he was depressed.

He went back to the drawing board. He revised the meals, cut back on entertainment and social events, and, as a conscientious worker, organized the conference with his double-cut budget.

You can imagine what happened. The salesmen were upset by the poor meals, the lack of snacks at cocktail time, and having to walk to meetings half a mile away in a second-rate hall. When they left, instead of being hyped up for the big sales campaign, they were griping about Easy Sales Corp.'s cheapness and lack of interest in the sales campaign. In fact, Phil Pockets—ace salesman—started a rumor that the company was on the skids and that commissions were going to be cut.

And then there was poor Will. Even with all his efforts to economize, he overran his budget. He faced the wrath of Harvey Harpooner, who had sunk a fine proposal with a single shot from the bow.

The following year Bill Brash was made conference chairman. But Bill knew how to use the Double-Cut Theory. He figured out what it would cost to put on the conference in style and developed his budget. Then he doubled the amount of everything.

Bill Brash presented the budget to Harvey Harpooner. Again Harvey took aim on the "fat" and scored a direct hit. He slashed and hacked the budget to pieces. What a manager!! When he had cut the budget literally in half, he called in Bill Brash to upbraid him for his extravagance and triumphantly produced the emaciated budget. Bill Brash acquiesced and Harvey Harpooner saw a dejected Bill walk out his office door. Once out the door, a broad grin came across Bill's face. A spring was in his step. Lo and behold, the bottom-line figure was exactly what Bill needed to put on a great conference—with a little to spare. With that extra, he bought gifts for the salesmen to commemorate the conference.

When the salesmen left the conference, they were filled with enthusiasm. They talked about what a great company they worked for, how things were looking up, and that the products introduced during the conference were sure to sell if they all got busy. To this day, Harvey Harpooner is talking about the fantastic (and cheap) conference Bill Brash put on. Bill became somewhat of a hero to management because, somehow, he put on that outstanding conference and even returned a few dollars to the company coffers.

There are some simple lessons to be learned from this example:

—Always ask for twice as much as you will need, on the assumption that your boss will cut the request in half.

—In the long run, management will remember your success, not the real cost of the project.

—The Double-Cut Theory permits your manager to fulfill his function of cutting out the fat without destroying the operation.

—The proper use of the Double-Cut Theory allows your boss

to answer "How come this project is so expensive?" with "I have cut the budget in half."

The fact is that, if you want to be successful and happy in your job, you had better begin asking for twice as much as you actually need to do the job. Even so, the Double-Cut Theory is not for everything. It is best used:

—In situations when it appears you or others would personally enjoy the result, such as conferences, training seminars, and so forth.

—When you make requests for help or for equipment that will make your job easier and require less overtime.

The Double-Cut Theory belongs in everyone's repertoire. Use it wisely and only when appropriate—but use it!

Moral:
By doubling your budget, you will double all the fun.
Management can make its cut and yet your project's done.

MAN ON THE MOON THEORY

OR

If It Can't Be Done, Spend Enough to Do It

Theory in brief:
Management believes that any obstacle can be hurdled or
any goal met
if sufficient resources are committed to the effort.

Apple pie, motherhood, and Old Glory are the American way. How we love the home run, the bomb in football, the breakaway in hockey, the clean knockout, and when good triumphs over evil. "Shoot for the moon," we shout. "We have nothing to fear but fear itself" is our slogan.

The country cheered when in the early 1960s President

John F. Kennedy announced to the American people, "We will have a man on the moon by the end of the decade." We did, too. How could such a feat be accomplished? It was easy. All that was needed was to overwhelm all obstacles with resources. "Damn the torpedoes, full speed ahead!"

Since that time, the American people in general, and American business in particular, have come to believe that no challenge is too great, no accomplishment beyond man's grasp. The New Deal, the Fair Deal, the Great Society! They are all attainable if we want them badly enough.

How can the concept of putting a man on the moon be used to help manage management? My friend, it is not easy. Just as putting a man on the moon was not easy. It took dedication and resources, work and resources, planning and resources, faith and resources, hope and resources, and just about anything else and resources. Get the point? Do you see those words written in the sky? WE CAN OVERCOME—WITH RESOURCES.

There are just two uses of the Man on the Moon Theory: (1) when you want to do something; and (2) when you don't want to do something.

What is important to remember is that management really believes anything is possible in any time frame *if* they allocate enough resources to the task. Let's look in on a scene that illustrates management's viewpoint:

Harvey Harpooner says to Will Workman, "Will, we must have that report ready on Monday morning." Since it is 3 P.M. on Friday, Will says, "Mr. Harpooner, there just isn't enough time. I don't have enough people. I'm sorry, but to be realistic, it just can't be done."

What is Harvey Harpooner thinking about Will? The Man on the Moon Theory states that, since anything is possible (if you allocate enough resources), Will Workman must be incompetent if he says it can't be done. That's just what Harvey Harpooner is thinking. Of course, Will is thinking that working overtime, double time, and supertime is impractical and that it just can't be so important. His real problem is that he doesn't understand the Man on the Moon Theory.

Harvey Harpooner is headed for Bill Brash's office. He tells Bill, "We need that SNAP report on Monday morning for the board meeting." Bill Brash realizes this is an unreasonable request, but he immediately says, "Okay, Mr. Harpooner, what time Monday morning do you need it?" When Harvey tells Bill he needs it about 8:45 A.M., Bill puts the Man on the Moon Theory to work.

"Mr. Harpooner," says Bill, "I figure I need three people to help me and your secretary's assistance all weekend." Bill makes this brash suggestion knowing that with that much help he could get out two SNAP reports by Monday morning. He also knows Harvey Harpooner's secretary will be furious if she has to work and that Harvey will regret making her work this weekend.

Now Bill Brash has made Harvey Harpooner count the cost. If he wants that report bad enough, he will provide the support. If it was a whim, Harvey might say, "Let me think about it," and rearrange the meeting for Tuesday or Wednes-

51

day morning. But Bill would never say it can't be done. Management just won't believe that. In any case, Bill will be a more valued employee than Will even if it turns out that neither produces the report by Monday morning.

So, remember Neil Armstrong. Management does. The first thing that will go through your manager's mind if you say it can't be done is "Tell it to Neil."

The Man on the Moon Theory also works if *you* want to do something badly and *management* is balking. Challenge management to put a man on the moon. Say something like:

—If our competition does it first, we're in real trouble.

—What could be more important than . . .

—If we pull it off, we'll all be promoted.

—If anybody can do it, you can.

As a subordinate you must understand the way management thinks and use it to your advantage if you want to manage management efficiently.

Moral:
Management expects of you success, and nothing less, sir.
The answer lies in spending more, or finding your successor.

RATHOLE THEORY

OR

Out of Sight, Out of Mind

Theory in brief:
Whatever funds or effort are expended will not be counted
in future evaluations——they're down the rathole.

The Rathole Theory is the cornerstone of corporate finance, government spending, and family budgeting. Yet few know the theory by name. Great economists such as Adam Smith and John Maynard Keynes developed theories of economics upon which government leaders debate. Great centers of learning such as the University of Pennsylvania have prepared elaborate models on spending. All are unnecessary. When you've said "rathole," you've said it all.

To see how the Rathole Theory works, let's first consider a typical domestic rathole—your TV set. Let's say your set cost $369 three years ago and is paid for. With any luck, a TV set may last three years without any appreciable problems. At the end of that period, you have a choice. Buy a new set or start repairing the old one.

One night during your favorite nighttime trivia, the set goes out. The repairman estimates that about $60 will fix it. What should you do? The typical citizen will reason: a new set will now cost $569, and it will only cost $60 to repair this one; therefore, I'll save money and spend just $60. You do, and the set comes to life again. With a sigh of relief and a Scotch in your hand, you settle back for another three years of TV.

Two months later, TV trouble is back. This time, your smiling repairman estimates that for $84.50 he can make it as good as new. The Rathole Theory says you'll ignore all previous expenditures and compare the cost of a new set, $569, against the cost of repairing the old set, $84.50. In most people's minds, what is spent is "down the rathole" and therefore not considered.

What will your decision be? If you are a typical rathole filler, it will be "Fix 'er up." The old set—getting older every day—has really cost you $144.50 in two months. And it's very likely that your repair bills will increase as the months go by. Never mind! When the set goes bad again, just say "rathole" and fix it.

How does this theory work in business? And how can you use it to manage management? Denny Dart and Harvey Harpooner can help us.

Denny has clashed frequently with the controller, Harvey Harpooner, over the costs of electronic data processing projects. Mr. Harpooner is determined to hold the line on what he considers to be frivolous projects. In fact, he issued an edict to this effect at the staff meeting just when Denny Dart was about to submit the proposal for his pet—a job-scheduling project for the data processing department.

Denny's dilemma is that if he were to present all the facts, it would be a break-even project at best. More than likely, the costs would exceed the benefits. In view of Mr. Harpooner's attitude, what can Denny do? It is time to use the Rathole Theory.

If Denny presents the proposal accurately, it will show that the system will cost $50,000 to develop and will save a maximum of $50,000 in reduced labor costs. Mr. Harpooner is not going to approve an unimpressive proposal like that no matter how much good it may do the company.

Denny knows the Rathole Theory. So he decides to use it in two phases. Phase 1 requires Denny to work up an irrefutable, optimistic proposal showing that the project will cost only $40,000. He does this and shows that the company will save $10,000 by approving his proposal. Mr. Harpooner doesn't need a calculator to know this will be a 25 percent return on investment. He is trapped. He must approve the project.

Phase 2 of the Rathole Theory comes into play when the $40,000 is spent. Denny Dart is prepared. He's like the con man moving the cups around so you can't tell which cup the pea is under. Denny tells Mr. Harpooner the sad story of how this and that caused him to run out of funds before the project was completed. "But look here, Mr. Harpooner," says Denny, deftly moving the cups, "for just another $10,000 I can save the company $50,000."

In case you have forgotten, that's the same $50,000 that Denny proposed to save on the original $40,000 investment. Nice move, Denny. Now, how does Mr. Harpooner look at it? He reasons that if he doesn't spend the $10,000, he'll lose $50,000. "Wow," he says to himself, "I can realize a 500 per-cent return on an investment of $10,000." Clearly, Mr. Har-pooner doesn't know which cup the pea is under. "You've got it, Denny," says H. H., thinking what a wise move he has made.

Pray tell, dear reader, how do *you* appraise the per-formance of Denny Dart? Did he get what he wanted? Is he a genius for earning the company a 500 percent return on its in-vestment? Should he be promoted or fired?

Knowing what you do, you may vote to toss him down the nearest elevator shaft. Knowing what I do about manage-ment, I bet he gets a promotion. The old rathole seldom fails. Out of sight, out of mind.

Okay, economists, eat your hearts out. The cat's out of the bag. Forget supply and demand. Forget cost of living, gross national product, and all that stuff. Forget historical costs. The power of positive thinking, using only future costs, makes everything so much more beautiful in its own way.

Moral:
Historical costs are a thing of the past
Supply and demand don't count.
Management's concern is for today,
So ask for any amount.

FUDGE FACTOR THEORY

Theory in brief:
To make estimated amounts match actual amounts,
add a fudge factor.

Estimates, budgets, and quotas are usually assigned by management. But they must be achieved by subordinates. Even when subordinates develop the figures, they are derived from rules laid down by management. That's why estimates, budgets, and quotas are a plague to all subordinates.

The subordinate's task is to explain the variances between estimated amounts and actual amounts. This gap can always be explained by the fudge factor. Here is the infallible fudge factor formula:

Estimated amount plus or minus fudge factor equals actual amount.

Let's look at a business situation in which the subordinate does not understand the Fudge Factor Theory. Randy

Rightman is in charge of projects A, B, and C, each with a budget of $10,000.

Project A winds up with an overrun of 10 percent and costs $11,000. Project B ends up costing 20 percent less than budget, or $8,000. Project C finishes with a 10 percent overrun and costs $11,000.

What is the net result? Randy had three projects with a total budget of $30,000, and he completed the three projects at an actual cost of $30,000. Did Randy Rightman do a good job? Of course not! Two of Randy's projects were out of control and ran over budget. Conclusion? Randy is a poor project manager. Randy's *real* problem is that he doesn't use fudge factors.

Let's see how Phil Pockets handles three similar projects. His projects A, B, and C are also budgeted at $10,000 each. Phil quickly notices that projects A and C are beginning to overrun their budgets. However, Project B is running under budget. Immediately, Phil applies the Fudge Factor Theory. One thousand dollars from each of Project A and C costs are "fudged" into Project B. When the three projects are finished, they fall within their individual budgets for a net total of $30,000. Did Phil do a good job? The controller, Harvey Harpooner, is so elated that he gives Phil a promotion. After all, who can beat a record of three out of three? Phil's batting .1000 in Harvey's book.

Since fudge factors are so important, we had better discuss what they are and how they work. They are adjustments, plugs, errors, unknown differences, and similar items that cause actual amounts to equal estimated amounts. Engineers, accountants, and purchasing agents have been using fudge factors for centuries.

There are two schools of thought on fudge factors. One says that fudge factors should be built into the estimated amounts beforehand. This means that, if you think you can complete a project for $10,000, you add a 20 percent fudge factor—making your estimate $12,000. You have just allowed for inflation, mistakes, or poor addition. If you think you can sell 400 items, estimate that you can sell 300. The difference of 100 items is the fudge factor. You have just allowed for a recession, an unforeseen illness, or poor salesmanship.

The second school of thought on fudge factors says you begin with a realistic estimate and add fudge factors as the day of reckoning approaches. The fudge factor must be appropriate for the situation. Phil Pockets shifted costs between accounts. Engineers and accountants specialize in this. Salesmen hold back sales and turn them in during critical periods when they fail to meet established quotas.

The beauty of the fudge factor is that, when you use it, you are virtually assured of success because you have hedged or fudged your bets. Management loves subordinates who consistently bring projects in under budget or who consistently exceed quotas. Use the fudge factor and you will be loved by management.

Let's examine some fudge factor techniques so you will have several to choose from when the occasion arises.

Underestimate fudge. Deliberately underestimate a quota so that it is easy to achieve or exceed.

Overestimate fudge. When submitting cost estimates, add a 20 percent fudge factor to be sure you don't run over budget.

Shifting cost fudge. If projects are running over or under, shift costs so all accounts come out on or under budget.

Plug fudge. If some detail causes the total to be over budget or exceed the control amount, plug in the difference so that it reconciles. For example, if a checking account doesn't reconcile, change the amount of one of the checks and it will.

Changing-condition fudge. When you find you cannot meet the budget or goal, blame an acceptable condition. Recessions, inflationary periods, war, strikes, and natural disasters are acceptable.

Next-year fudge. If sales or costs are not what they should be, shift them from one accounting period to another. For example, if you have not met your sales quota, ask your best customer to place an order before year's end for delivery as needed. You get your sales bonus, your customer gets a quantity discount, and your sales manager is deliriously happy. This technique can be used to overpurchase supplies to spend excess funds or divert variable costs to the following year.

Quality fudge. If you can't adjust the price, plug the difference, or shift the cost, you can always change the quality. This is very effective fudge. For example, if available funds will not permit you to buy new equipment, buy used. If the specs call for three coats of paint and you don't have the money, apply only two coats. (CAUTION: The *Titanic* may have been built using this fudge factor.)

These fudge factors are the subordinate's friends. In any given situation, these or other fudges you may ingeniously concoct will always equal the difference between the actual amount and the estimated amount.

While the ethics of some of these fudges may be questionable, they work. Even if your conscience won't let you use them, you ought to understand them.

Moral:
For meeting a goal that just won't budge,
Use the friendly factor known as fudge.

GROUP

2

Theories Designed to Make Management Consider You Worthy of Promotion

---

BOTH ENDS OF THE CLOCK THEORY

OR

How to Get Ahead Through the Judicious Use of Twelve Minutes a Day

---

Theory in brief:
To some managers, what happens during the day matters
far less than whether you arrive and leave on time.

Ken Census, supervisor for Easy Sales Corp., is meeting with his boss, Ivan Kingman, to discuss raises for his employees. At the moment, the discussion centers on two secretaries.

Cindy Sharp is a very efficient secretary who completes her work quickly and with few errors. She also points out problems to Ken so that he can handle them before they become costly. Cindy volunteers to work overtime at the office or at home during the crunches. In short, Cindy is Ken's best secretary.

Nancy Numb is a plodding worker. She is not particularly accurate and turns out far less work than Cindy. Nancy absolutely refuses to work overtime anywhere. However, you can set your watch by her. She arrives three minutes before starting time, takes exactly one hour for lunch, never leaves before closing time, and keeps busy all day.

Ken says, "I'd like to see Cindy get a good raise this time, Mr. Kingman. She deserves it."

Kingman replies, "You know, Ken, I've noticed that Cindy has poor work habits. The other morning I dropped by to check on your department and she wasn't at her desk. It was 8:34. I've also noticed that she leaves a few minutes early from time to time. And to top it off, Ken, she overstays her lunch hour playing bridge."

Needless to say, Ken is going to find it tough to get Cindy much of a raise. Ivan is rating Cindy on the nontechnical aspects of her job. This is standard procedure for supervisors with little experience or knowledge of technical jobs.

After Ivan tells Ken he will keep Cindy in mind (a statement that means he will promptly forget her), Ken goes on to discuss Nancy. He has hardly mentioned her name when Ivan says, "Ken, I've noticed Nancy. She's a real workhorse. She's always at work on time, never goofs off on her lunch hour, and I've never known her to leave early. I know you want a good raise for Nancy and I'll see to it that she gets it. We need more workers like her."

With all her efficiency, initiative, and willing spirit,

Cindy has one important thing to learn from Nancy: how to manage management.

Nancy is a master at applying the Both Ends of the Clock Theory. As a result, she manages Ivan Kingman masterfully.

If Cindy would just recognize that her raises depend on the judicious use of twelve minutes a day, she would make more money with less effort. The Both Ends of the Clock Theory merely requires Cindy to arrive three minutes early, leave three minutes late and return three minutes early from lunch, and leave three minutes after the closing hour.

That's how Nancy gets her raises.

The Both Ends of the Clock Theory unequivocally states that what happens between the starting and closing hour is far less important than starting and finishing the workday on time.

Management textbooks extol competence and hard work as the two characteristics upon which advancement is based.

Don't believe it. In actual practice, advancement is more often related to two factors: (1) strict adherence to company policies and procedures, and (2) people factors. A checklist of criteria under each of these factors is given below.

If you want steady raises and promotions, you must recognize that you are likely to be rated by your supervisor on the nontechnical aspects of your job. By finding out which superficial criteria you are being rated on, you can be sure to excel in them.

Any employee who is willing to apply the Both Ends of the Clock Theory will find it a real help in managing management.

You may turn twelve minutes a day into real money. Try it.

Nontechnical Rating Criteria Checklist
Strict Adherence to Company Policies and Procedures

- ☐ Starting work on time
- ☐ Taking a short hour for lunch
- ☐ Never leaving until after closing time
- ☐ Never parking in the boss's parking spot
- ☐ Looking busy
- ☐ Ad infinitum

People Factors

- ☐ Ability to get along
- ☐ Friendliness with those outside your department
- ☐ Getting customers to say a good word about you
- ☐ Having blood relations or in-laws in strategic positions
- ☐ Seniority
- ☐ Good looks, good health, right age, etc.
- ☐ Education
- ☐ Having the right wife (the right husband doesn't help unless your boss is a woman)
- ☐ Engaging in highly visible and acceptable community activities
- ☐ Proper political identification
- ☐ A fashionable religion

□ Being black or white (as the case may be)
□ Having illustrious relatives (or a long family tree with the
   right roots)

NOTE: To use this checklist effectively, you must determine your boss's ranking of each criterion.

Moral:
If you want a real good raise
And don't know how to get it,
Do the things your boss will praise
You'll never once regret it.

BLUE MOLD THEORY

OR

Don't Tell Me How to Do It, I'm Moldier Than You

Theory in brief:
Like cheese, people and equipment are not considered
valuable until they grow a thick coat of mold.

Perry's Perfect Principle
The longer you work for a company, the more mold you
accumulate, the more attractive you are
to the typical manager.

Perry's Perilous Parallel
You must know more; you've been here longer.

Remember that feeling of uncertainty when you began your
last job? The neophyte feeling that lasts for days, weeks,
months, and even years in some organizations? Not only was

your position new, but so were the people, the surroundings, and the operating procedures. Sooner or later, however, you began to build confidence in your ability to perform.

According to the Blue Mold Theory, at this point you had been there just long enough to accumulate a little mold. To help you see why, let's consider the cheese connoisseur.

When visiting a gourmet cheese shop, the true connoisseur does not merely consider taste. That's for lesser lights like you and me. The connoisseur realizes that the mold-growing process is essential to the development of flavor and texture in cheese. He is sure that under the mold lies an exquisite flavor. The novice cheese tester is tempted to judge the quality of cheese by mere taste. He does not consider mold an essential to quality.

The problem comes when the connoisseur will not test cheese without mold. Says he, "Perdonemeau, monsieure, the cheese without mold c'est miserable." Meanwhile, he passes up many delicious cheeses in the process. In other words, to some the proof is in the eating. To others, it's in the molding.

The presence or absence of mold determines how employees are viewed in many organizations. Oftentimes people are judged not by what they can do, but by the amount of blue mold they have accumulated. (Why blue? Because that describes how employees feel sitting around waiting for mold to grow. For until it does, they will not be entrusted with any worthwhile project.)

Of course, if you manage to survive the gestation period, the Blue Mold Theory may prove either advantageous or disadvantageous, depending on how moldy the other employees are. Your mold can accumulate very quickly in a department with a high rate of employee turnover.

When management is faced with a decision (heaven forbid), they generally take the easiest way out. What's that? They decide on the basis of mold. For example, Jane Withered and Norm New are discussing the amount of time required to finish Project SNAFU. Norm has accumulated only a few scattered spots of mold in his few months, while Jane Withered is completely covered with inches of blue mold. Norm presents some impressive statistics, but Jane speaks with historical authority about Project LATE, Project ABANDONED, and so forth. Management can't resist that mold. They side with it almost every time.

The Blue Mold Theory applies a number of ways in business. For instance, a data processing manager may be trying to decide between International Big Machines Corp. equipment and one of the new, innovative kids on the block. If the data processing manager decides to go with Sweet 'n Healthy Systems Corp. and things don't work out, he will be blamed for making a bad decision. On the other hand, if the data processing manager chooses moldy International Big Machines equipment and things don't work out, management will feel that he had done everything possible to assure the success of the project. As far as management is concerned, blue mold and blue chip are synonymous.

Management's viewpoint toward blue mold equipment and personnel leads to the following conclusions:

If you are uncertain as to which product or person is best for the job, make your choice based on blue mold thickness. If the project fails, management will consider it to have been an impossible task.

Your probability of winning an argument is proportional to mold thickness. In other words, if you are short on mold, you are sure to lose.

If you go against the Blue Mold Theory, be prepared to work like hell to make the project successful. If you don't, your decision against blue mold will come back to haunt you.

Take this advice, my friend. Grow mold as quickly as possible and use existing blue mold around you to help manage management. It's better than penicillin—there are no side effects.

Moral:
The way your boss rejects your thoughts
may sizzle and may burn you.
But till your mold has grown quite deep,
he'll fear to trust so spurn you.

GLASS HOUSE THEORY

Theory in brief:
Since everybody's watching, do what *they* think is best.
After all, the attitudes and opinions of others must be
more important than doing what is right.

Managers are great believers in the Glass House Theory. They are convinced that everyone is watching them and that nothing escapes anyone's notice. Their philosophy is "People who live in glass houses shouldn't make controversial decisions." This thinking permeates every level of management.

While you can argue the wisdom of trying to make decisions that please everyone, you cannot deny that everybody is watching management's actions. Subordinates are watching; peer-level managers are watching; and certainly higher-level managers are watching. Consequently, the first thing a manager thinks of when faced with a decision is "What will *they* think of my decision?"

The Glass House Theory has always been with us. Like Pavlov's dog, we are conditioned to respond to it. As youngsters, whenever we sat down to eat, we were told with a well-directed nudge of the elbow, "Watch your manners. People will see how sloppy you are!" As teen-agers, our lives were almost totally dominated by the Glass House Theory. We were told to get a haircut, you look like a freak. We were told to get that shirt off, what will the neighbors think. We were told to get some shoes on, Aunt Ida's coming. Yes, we lived in glass houses and still do.

The Glass House Theory is known by other names too, such as "Watch your manners," "Don't break with tradition," and "It's not our custom." By any other name, this rose smells. It limits our creativity, stunts our intellectual growth, and pours us into a mold of conformity. Think about it. Would you attend a cocktail party wearing sneakers? Would you admit you voted for Nixon? Would you announce that you got your diploma from the school of hard knocks when talking to a group of MBAs? Why the negative answers? Because the Glass House Theory has got you.

No wonder, then, that managers make glass house decisions. Humans do many things that seem ridiculous on the surface but make sense when you realize they are done in a glass house. For example, soldiers will march until they faint dead away because they fear the criticism of their superiors or their peers. Members of organizations attend boring meetings only because they feel someone will look askance at them if they don't. Managers and supervisors will stay a few minutes after quitting time to impress watching subordinates.

If we are to manage management successfully, we must learn how the Glass House Theory works and how to make it work *for* us rather than *against* us. To see the theory in action, consider what happened to Will Workman.

Will did an outstanding job for Easy Sales Corp. last year. He worked extra hours, used creative approaches to problems, and generally put out the something extra that turns an average performance into an outstanding one. If Will Workman ever deserved a raise, it was this year. Did he get one? No! Why not?

Harvey Harpooner, Will's boss, explained it this way: "Will, I know what a great job you did last year and I know you deserve a good raise. And I would give you one too, but my hands are tied. Ivan Kingman has set the guidelines for salary increases and, as guardian of the corporate purse strings, I wouldn't dare violate the rules and set a wrong example. But don't think I lack appreciation for your good work. I'll take care of you next year, ole buddy."

Ever hear that refrain? Yes, it's an old and popular tune, sung by managers who live in glass houses. The same tune is sung with new words when it comes to making decisions to spend money for needed equipment. Wendy Watch had that problem with her boss, Tom Tough.

Wendy spends a lot of her time typing form letters in answer to various inquiries. She knows that word processing equipment could save the company money by doubling or tripling her output and, at the same time, do the job perfectly. There is not one piece of word processing equipment in Easy Sales Corp., although there are many uses for it. This is what dooms Wendy's request. When asked about purchasing a machine, Tom reasons, "I'll be the first to spend that much money for that kind of equipment. What will my boss think? What will Ivan Kingman think? What if it doesn't pan out? I'll be criticized." What result will this glass house thinking have on Tom's decision? Unless he is willing to base his decision on logic and facts, Tom will succumb to his fear of popular opinion—because he lives in a glass house.

Since it isn't likely we'll ever suppress the glass house syndrome, we had better learn to live with it or, better still, turn it to our advantage. This will often work for the good of your employer, because many times the opinion of the watchers is not clear—or correct. In such cases, people make incorrect decisions based on what they *think* those peering into their glass houses believe should be done.

To see how to make the Glass House Theory work for you, let's view an instant replay of Will Workman's conversation with Harvey Harpooner, the controller.

Before Will can turn this situation around to his benefit, he must understand the Personal Dow-Jones Theory. It simply states that if your personal stock is to rise in the company, you must not leave decisions affecting your wages or promotions to the boss. You must manage management. This requires your personal involvement. You must step in and make the right things happen.

Now, let's see how Will Workman could have approached Mr. Harpooner if he understood the interplay of the Glass House and Personal Dow-Jones theories. At an opportune moment, Will approaches Mr. Harpooner to discuss the upcoming raises.

"Harvey, I'd like to talk to you about the salary increases for this year and the guidelines Mr. Kingman has given you covering these raises," says Will in a very positive, businesslike manner. "Sure, Will," replies Harpooner. "Glad to discuss it with you." The fact is that this is one subject neither Harvey Harpooner nor any other manager wants to discuss with any subordinate.

To keep Harpooner from bolting out of sheer panic, Will does not discuss his personal situation but describes the case of another employee that fits Will's description to a tee. Will says, "We've got a few people in this department who have done an outstanding job. Randy Rightman, for example. He has put in a lot of extra time working on projects, he takes a creative approach to his work, and has put out that something extra that has turned what would have been an ordinary job into an extraordinary one." Sound familiar?

Will goes on. "Harvey, I know what a problem it is for you to compensate Randy for his outstanding effort within the guidelines Mr. Kingman has set. He knows that very few do an outstanding job, so he sets the salary guidelines with this in mind. Nevertheless, Mr. Kingman will expect those few to be properly rewarded. I don't think some of the others in positions like yours realize what Mr. Kingman expects in this regard. You and I both know that Mr. Kingman wants every employee to perform like Randy and the few others like him. At any rate, I thought I'd let you know that in my department just Randy and Wendy Watch are the ones I would single out for special treatment. This should stimulate the others to imitate their good example."

Now, with this expanded viewpoint, and realizing Ivan Kingman has his nose pressed against the glass in his house, Harvey Harpooner will feel free—even obligated—to make a few exceptions to the general guidelines for salary increases. This should include Will Workman, since he is obviously in the "outstanding worker" category.

Since the Glass House Theory is so prevalent throughout the business world, you owe it to yourself to understand and use it to manage frightened management.

Moral
Most business decisions are made in glass houses,
Denying the logic that your boss espouses.

PERSONAL DOW-JONES
THEORY

Theory in brief:
**Maximize your personal worth to your boss at evaluation
time.**

When Will Workman was eighteen, he enlisted in the Army.
Will was young and ambitious. He believed his Dad who said,
"Work hard and you will get ahead!" Will looked forward to
rapid promotion through the ranks.

When Phil Pockets was eighteen, he was drafted into
the Army. Phil was lazy. He didn't believe in the work ethic,
and he didn't care if he got ahead. But he too looked forward
to rapid promotion through the ranks. Phil and Will entered
the service on the same day.

Five years later, they met. Will knew Phil before he
was drafted. He was amazed to see master sergeant's stripes

on Phil's arm. Will Workman's single PFC stripe looked sick. "Where did I go wrong?" he lamented. The answer is simple: Phil Pockets learned the secret of the Personal Dow-Jones Theory. Will Workman just worked like a dog. What *is* the secret Phil learned? Let's start at the beginning.

In 1897 Dow-Jones began to publish an industrial average of stocks so investors could readily see price trends of stocks and bonds. It was successful, since investors needed to know whether stock prices were rising or falling in order to capitalize on the time-proven axiom "Buy low, sell high." Like the stock market, people too have a "Dow-Jones" average, which we refer to as the personal Dow-Jones.

A worker's personal Dow-Jones is determined by a process known as "performance evaluation." The industrial Dow-Jones average is obtained by averaging the prices of common stock from thirty industrial firms. Your boss obtains your personal Dow-Jones by evaluating some fifteen work characteristics. In most organizations, this ritual is conducted once a year at the time promotions and raises are given. That's the moment to push your personal Dow-Jones as high as possible. Meanwhile, back to Master Sergeant Phil Pockets and Private First Class Will Workman.

Let's find out how Phil manipulated his personal Dow-Jones average to make master sergeant in five years while Will plodded to the lowly rank of PFC. Soon after Phil was drafted, Master Sergeant Denny Dart took a liking to him. They were two of a kind. This was fortunate, for Denny knew the ropes. It was Denny who taught Phil the secret of the personal Dow-Jones.

As Denny explained it to Phil, "What you do when you are assigned to a new position is make your personal Dow-Jones drop dramatically. You do this through poor work, poor attitudes, and poor personal habits." "Won't that get you demoted?" asked Phil. "I'm coming to that," Denny continued. "When your personal Dow-Jones drops, it's just like the stock market. You can't let it drop too far or the owner will sell. So you've got to watch it." "But won't the Captain get after you?" asked a bewildered Phil. "Of course, that's just what you want," said Denny. "He'll have a heart-to-heart talk with you like 'Shape up or ship out!' " Phil asked, "What do you do then?"

"I shape up," says Denny. "I listen to everything the Captain says and I do exactly what he wants me to do. By evaluation day, my value in the boss's eyes, or my personal Dow-Jones, is way up. Now the Captain isn't selling. He's thinking, 'I've got a gem here. The best thing to do is to promote him.' By working hard just a few weeks before evaluation time, I get a promotion every year." "But I work hard all the time," moans Phil. "And I only got one promotion in five years." "It's because your stock just edges up so slowly it's unnoticed by the Captain," Denny explained. "You, as a stock, are in a holding position. The Captain won't get rid of you but you're not a hot item either. You'd do better by dramatically manipulating your personal Dow-Jones once a year than by slowly inching up all the time."

Denny's right, Phil. See that arm full of stripes.

Similarities abound between the industrial Dow-Jones average and your personal Dow-Jones average. Think for a moment. What affects stock prices? Why is it a company can increase earnings and yet experience a decline in the price of their stock? The answer is that performance is only *one* criterion for evaluating a stock. Prices are also affected by national unemployment figures, foreign exchange rates, the Federal Reserve discount policy, statements made by the President, how large stock funds are reacting to the stock, favorable or unfavorable newspaper stories about the company, and even the time of year. Why, then, should we think that our personal Dow-Jones is affected only by how well we do our job? It's not!

Here are fifteen criteria by which you will be judged. Any one or all of them will affect your personal Dow-Jones average.

Criteria

1. Getting to your work station on time.
2. Saying, "you're right, boss," at the right time.
3. Making your boss's whims your Number One priority.
4. Keeping the right company.
5. Completing administrative trivia on time.
6. Completing projects on time.
7. Completing projects within budget.
8. Looking important.
9. Acting important.
10. Talking about the right things.
11. Living by the organization's rules.
12. Making sure your subordinates live by the rules.

13. Supporting the right causes.
14. Supporting your boss's position on anything.
15. Staying at your work station until quitting time.

Your personal advancement is too important to leave in the hands of your superior. Watch out for statements such as, "Work hard and the company will take care of you" and, "Let me worry about your future." Bull! You'd better have those statements translated. In the language of truth, the first statement means, "Keep your nose to the grindstone and your mouth shut." The second statement means, "Don't bug me about tomorrow, just do what you're told today!" Brutal facts, but true. Those who manage their own careers get ahead, while the Will Workmans of the business world work their lives away with few rewards.

Let's take a look at some of the concepts Denny used to move his personal Dow-Jones up at the critical time. You can learn a lot from this.

Don't waste your good ideas. Save them for the period just before evaluation time.

Don't give the boss bad news until raises have been distributed. If you tell him you've overrun the budget or fouled something up just before evaluation, your stock is going to plummet. So will your raise.

Practice the Both Ends of the Clock and the Paper Avalanche Theories just before performance evaluation time.

Get your peers to praise you to the boss during performance

evaluation. (This won't be hard unless they too understand the Personal Dow-Jones Theory.)

Become your own spokesman at performance evaluation time. Sometimes the investor isn't watching the Dow- Jones average.

Now, not all bosses are so callous. You should closely analyze yours. Is he the type of person you want directing your life? Is he the type of person you'd be willing to bet your career on? Is he the type of person who will fight for *your* best interest? If not, take over your own career development. Spend time on it. Cultivate it. And move your personal Dow-Jones average to its zenith at performance evaluation time. If you do, your boss will be willing to invest more in you—and that means more take home pay, greater prestige, and a better position.

Moral:
By leaving your raise up to your boss;
You won't get more, you'll take a loss.

SEVENTY-THIRTY
THEORY

Theory in brief:
Spend seventy percent of your time working,
thirty percent lining up your next job.

Parkinson's Law states that work expands so as to fill the available time. He developed this law after analyzing statistics published by the British Admiralty on its activities during the first quarter of the twentieth century. The study showed that while the number of ships in commission dropped from sixty-two in 1914 to twenty in 1928, the number of Admiralty officials increased from 2,000 to 3,569. Since that study, it is generally accepted that people will use whatever time is available to do the job at hand. According to Parkinson, if a worker has five hours available to do a job that should take only two hours, he will take five hours to do that job.

Parkinson saw that work and time are not necessarily related. This means that neither your job nor your performance is evaluated on the amount of work accomplished in a given time. An exception to this would be piecework. However, in most cases, job security does not depend on output. As Parkinson saw in the British Admiralty, the work can actually decrease while the staff increases. Yet everyone keeps busy doing the available work, whatever that may be.

Now to the 70/30 Theory.

This theory states that an individual should use only seventy percent of his time doing his job and thirty percent acting as his own public relations man or press agent. If you follow Parkinson's law and expand your work to fill one hundred percent of your time, you will find that sooner or later your boss will find something else for you to do (see Spinning Plate Theory). That is not good. Your boss will seldom have you do something you want to do.

We're not telling you to volunteer for work. Millions of GI's learned never to volunteer. The sergeant used to ask, "Anybody here know how to type?" The unfortunate who raised his hand found himself peeling potatoes . . . of every type. Volunteering is a no-no in business. Volunteering means you have nothing to do. Volunteering means your job is not important. Volunteering means you are not even clever enough to invoke Parkinson's law.

Visualize this scene. Norman New goes into Tom Tough's office and says, "I'm out of work. What shall I do?" Does this make Tom happy? Does this endear Norman to him? Not at all. Norman becomes a source of irritation. All he has done is put Tom on the spot. Tom must give Norman something to do or Norm will wonder why he was hired in the first place. He may even ask Harvey Harpooner that question and get Tom in trouble. So Tom isn't going to let Norman New sit around doing nothing. He says, "Norman, go through the files and throw away all letters over three years old." Well, Norman, you asked for it. Instead of running out of work, you should have spent thirty percent of your time getting your next assignment lined up so you would have work you enjoyed.

Sam Smoothwater told Norman that he should judge the length of his next assignment by the time it will take him to locate the following job. For example, Sam figured it would take three weeks to line up another good project, so he allowed ten weeks to do the job Harvey Harpooner just gave him. You are much better off selecting your own future jobs than allowing your boss to come up with a "make work" assignment.

The only assignment Ivan Kingman was ever given on his way to the presidency was to fill out the job application form. From that moment on, Ivan plotted his own course to the top. He knew and practiced the 70/30 Theory. Even during the interview, Ivan spent thirty percent of his time figuring out what his first assignment would be.

Ivan had another bit of insight that helped him succeed in each new job he undertook. He realized that when you are the first one to do a job, your performance cannot be compared to someone else's. The first person to perform a feat gets into the Guinness Book of World Records. It *has* to be a world record, it's a first!

The only job Ivan took that had been done before was the presidency of Easy Sales Corp. And on the first day of that job, Ivan rewrote the job description. He knew that the best jobs are those for which *you* write the position guide.

The 70/30 Theory is like working your way through a maze. You spend seventy percent of your time walking and thirty percent of your time finding the next turn. The trick is never to hit a dead end. Spending thirty percent of your time looking for your next turn gives you time to backtrack and find your way out before it's too late.

So down with Parkinson and up with the 70/30 Theory! It'll keep you one step ahead of your boss in that maze that leads to better jobs, more money, and greater authority.

Moral:
Running out of work only leads to sorrow,
Without an assignment, there is no tomorrow.

TURN THE HERD THEORY

Theory in brief:
If a project is on the brink of disaster, you can
salvage a victory by turning the herd.

This, of all theories, is most admired by the crowd. It's a grandstand play. And it doesn't happen every day. In fact, you may only be able to turn the herd half a dozen times in a career. But even if you turn the herd only once, it will bring a sense of satisfaction you'll never forget.

Sports figures become heroes when they turn the herd. With his team down by 14 points in the final five minutes of the fourth quarter, a linebacker intercepts a pass and runs for a touchdown. On the next series of plays, the defense holds. With the score 14 to 7, the hyped-up team scores again . . . and yet again! The linebacker turned the herd and has become a hero. He's carried off the field on the shoulders of his teammates. His picture fills sports pages across the nation.

One key event can turn a situation around. Can this happen in business? Yes. Does it happen in business? Yes.

But if you are going to turn the herd, you must know when the big play is needed and give it the old college try. There isn't as much to lose as you may think. For instance, if the linebacker had missed the interception and the tight end had caught it and scored for the other team, it wouldn't have mattered much. The linebacker wouldn't have been blamed any more than if the pass had just gone incomplete. However, by anticipating the big play and giving it his all, the linebacker became a hero. If you make an all-out attempt for the big play and fail, often the worst that can happen is you get an "E" for effort. So look for your opportunity to turn the herd, and grab it.

To turn the herd, three conditions must exist:

1—You must be a part of the herd.
2—You must be among the leaders of the herd.
3—You must be working on an unquantifiable project.

Our idea of turning the herd in a typical Western movie is all wrong. We always see the cowboy in the white hat on the white horse, charging the herd from the opposite direction, firing both pistols wildly. In the movie, he turns the herd away from the cliff and becomes a hero. In real life, he gets ground to hamburger under the hooves of the herd as it continues on in the same direction.

The way to turn the herd is to turn the leaders. The rest

of the herd will blindly follow. That's the way it is in business. Ken Census got into a management position even though he's a nice guy. Such a thing would never have happened unless Ken had turned the herd. How did he do it?

Tom Tough gave Ken Census the assignment of organizing the annual office party. Tom didn't want anything to do with it because it had always been a "must-come, no-fun" affair. Tom thought this assignment might even end Ken's career at Easy Sales Corp. "Oh, well," thought Tom. "Not much lost. Nice guys always finish last." Since Ken sensed his situation was desperate, he decided to turn the herd. He carefully thought out his plan of attack. Before actually making his move to turn the herd, he would create the three conditions vital to success.

Become a part of the herd. Required to run with the herd, Ken began to sympathize with the rest of the cattle. He joined them in uttering such expressions as "I hate these parties," "Why me?" and "Why don't they just give us money instead?" Old Ken was trotting right alongside the rest of the beefers. Even though he was the planner of the annual event, he sounded like a victim.

Move to the head of the herd. Ken became the foremost griper of the group. He told Tom Tough that he didn't have enough time, enough talent, or enough money to put on a successful party. Since Ken complained the loudest about the party, he assumed a lead position in the herd.

Make the project unique. Ken thought long and hard about this one. Then he hit on an idea! The annual office party had always been held in a restaurant, where there was no room to move around. This inhibited activity and conversation. He would hold a catered party in his home. Nice move, Ken. Since this had never been tried before, Ken's party could be compared to no other. No matter how it turned out, it was one of a kind. Now Ken was ready to turn the herd.

He started out slowly. He began to say incredulously, "You know, the party just might turn out to be tolerable this year." Later he told Tom Tough, "I think the troops will have fun." Since everybody really wanted to have a good time, Ken's mood was contagious. After all, he was the biggest griper. If Ken thought it might work out, it just might! The herd started to follow Ken and turn from despair to delight. Ken had the ball and was running for a touchdown.

If you stop to think, you will remember all kinds of situations that looked bleak for a long time but suddenly took a turn for the better. It was because someone turned the herd. Remember the dress you didn't dare buy until your husband said, "Honey, you'd look great in that dress." You bought it even though it cost $110.95. How often has a child hated his toy until an older brother said, "That's a great toy. I wish I had one." What about the comedian who, dying on the stage, finally came up with an awful joke. He realized it was so bad he might as well admit it. He used that joke over and over until it became funny and delightful. These are all examples of turning the herd.

It's a wonderful theory, it's a fun theory, and best of all, it can be used by the Ken Censuses and the Will Workmans of the business world. Good, hard-working people are believable when they turn the herd. The Denny Darts and Phil Pocketses of the world have a difficult time getting the herd to follow them.

Try turning the herd. You'll like it.

Moral:

When the project's bad and the worst's occurred,
Put your thinking cap on and turn the herd.

ALIBI FILE THEORY

OR,

Why I Didn't Do What You Think I Ought to Have Done

Theory in brief:
Whether you do something or nothing, you'd better be
prepared to defend your position.

A group of middle-level executives are gathering for an important business meeting in one of the plushier conference rooms. A key decision is needed on a project that has had its share of problems.

Sam A. Stute, the project leader, will play a dominant role in the meeting even though his was only one of several departments involved in the project. As the group enters the conference room, notice the materials each person carries. Some come only with an open mind. Others carry agendas, scratch pads, and notebooks. Still others have folders containing previous minutes or correspondence relating to the project.

Our project leader, Sam, carries a bulging briefcase plus an armful of papers into the room. None of this is handout material. It is Sam's alibi file.

Sam had been around the organization for a number of years and has numerous battle scars to show for his involvement in other projects. He is quite familiar with overruns, missed budgets, and misappropriations of responsibility.

At this stage of the game, Sam's primary interest is not the success of the project, not meeting target dates or timetables, not meeting the real needs of the organization. Sam's main interest is in protecting Sam. Thus in the true spirit of PTA* is born the alibi file.

Sam's alibi file is quite simple: a file of alibis complete with an elaborate index system. The file includes correspondence, memos, and notes relating to the project and a generous sprinkling of Sam's "Memos for the Record." What do these memos contain? Documentation of conversations that others have long forgotten, what Sam thought the other people meant by what they said, what Sam was thinking when he heard them say it, as well as assumptions and conclusions that Sam deduced from any of these to support his plan of action or inaction.

Efficient filing and indexing are crucial to the success of an alibi file. After all, when Sam is pinned to the wall, in-

* Protect Thine Arse.

stant retrieval is essential if he is to call up just the right alibi for the occasion.

Let's take a look at a typical example of how the alibi file bailed Sam out when the going got rough.

Harvey Harpooner, controller, opens the meeting by saying, "Sam, when this project started, you said that it would contain items X and Y. As I see it, you have managed to produce only item Y. And that's my question. Why?"

Sam scurries through his file and with great dexterity extracts his notes on a conversation held eight months and three days ago with Freddie Fallguy at the coffee machine. "Here," says Sam, "is a note of what Freddie said on August 13, and I quote: 'The project is primarily designed to produce item Y.' From this conversation, Mr. Harpooner, I assumed that my efforts should be largely directed toward producing item Y.

"As a matter of fact," continues Sam, deftly dipping into his alibi file, "my memo for the record of October 20, which I have right here, shows that I called Freddie and told him that the project would, at a minimum, include item Y. He certainly knew that I was homing in on item Y, and that seemed to be his understanding of the project too," etc., etc.

As you can see, the alibi file is quite effective.

If you are placed in a situation where you are responsible for producing something, there is always the possibility that you may produce nothing. And there may be many reasons for this. As Murphy so eloquently put it, "Whatever can go wrong will, and at the worst possible moment." Or you may find that, as project leader, you have been assigned to a project doomed to certain failure. In such cases, the alibi file can be a strong ally.

However, alibi files are not without their disadvantages. All such files are very time-consuming and costly. It is not unusual for an alibi file to cost several thousand dollars. In some major projects, I have known alibi files to fill two file drawers, require the services of a full-time secretary, and cost an estimated $25,000. While this may seem a high price to pay, do not underestimate the value of an alibi file. If it contains the right kind of documentation, it can pull you out of just about any scrape.

However, before you decide to build an alibi file for your present project, you should consider the dangers inherent in its use:

—Since it consumes so much time, it often ensures the failure of the project.

—Keeping an alibi file may label you as an incompetent. (Nevertheless, your colleagues will find it very difficult to challenge you on your project's objectives and your actions to achieve them.)

—The use of an alibi file severely limits your opportunities for promotion because, though the file helps you to protect yourself, you may accomplish little else. (It does, however, protect your current position in the organization.)

Thus you should view the alibi file as a defensive weapon in the arena of managing management. It won't help you defeat the enemy, but it will protect you against a coup by your colleagues.

If you want to spend more time working than documenting yourself, perhaps a simple alibi pocket-finder will suffice. This is a small note pad which you can carry in your shirt pocket or purse. If you use that notebook often and accurately enough, you will eventually convince management and your co-workers that you know everything they or you ever said or did. That may just be enough to keep them off your back.

Moral:

If you want to be quite sure that never red your face is,
Build a file of alibis complete with names and places.

COMPANY PHOTOGRAPH
THEORY

Theory in brief:
It's not what you know, but who you're
seen with that counts.

A basic truth in business is, "It's not *what* you know, but *whom* you know." The Company Photograph Theory is derived from that truism. If you are photographed with the right people, it is assumed you know them or are on their side. Being photographed or associating with the wrong people can ruin your career. Why? Because as the old proverb says, if you go to bed with dogs, you'll wake up with fleas.

The Company Photograph Theory says that, if you stand with the right people in company photographs, their stardom will rub off on you. It may sound ridiculous, but it's true. And not all photographs are hanging on walls. The boss is always taking pictures with that sound, color, videotape device we call his eyes, ears, and brain. With whom does he see you eat lunch? Who are your friends in the organization? Are they the up-and-comers, or the downtrodden like Swann Songue? As distasteful as it may seem, the boss had better be taking pictures of you with the right people or you'll end up classified with the losers.

Take, for example, the selection of Easy Sales Corp.'s new vice president of customer relations. There were two good candidates for the job, Tom Tough and Randy Rightman. This position was considered vital to the continued growth of the company; it was quite a plum. The decision was to be made by Ivan Kingman, president and chairman of the board. In the loneliness of his luxuriously appointed office, Ivan was agonizing over the decision. As he paced the floor, he unconsciously gazed at some company photographs on his wall. In them were both Tom and Randy. In several, Randy was standing next to people like Swann Songue and Dee Endd, lovely people, but losers. On the other hand, Tom was standing next to Ivan's son and Harvey Harpooner, not very nice people—but winners. Without realizing why, Ivan suddenly made up his mind. "Of course," he thought, "Tom is right for the new post. He is a winner!"

The Company Photograph Theory works! Did Randy deserve to be classified with the losers and Tom with the winners? Not at all. But the hard fact is, deserved or not, they *were* classified because of the ones they associated with.

The Company Photograph Theory states that your career opportunities are directly related to the people with whom you associate. If you want to move up the hierarchical ladder, you must hitch your wagon to a star. Become that star's protégé, and you will move up with him. And, make no mistake about it, you must consciously decide whom to hitch to early in your career. Once the decision is made, you will be photographed with that person in management's mind.

No doubt you have heard those who are rising quickly in your organization referred to as "comers" or "rising stars." That's a misnomer. They are really "cabooses"! Why cabooses? Because these people are being pulled to the top by one or more powerful locomotives. If you are hooked onto the right locomotive you move right up the track. But if you get hooked onto an engine that has lost its power, like Swann Songue, you are going nowhere. And if your locomotive gets derailed, all the cars in back of it go off the track too—including you!

So, when you join an organization, don't hook onto the first locomotive coming by. Don't spend your time with the "good ole boys." And don't hook up with a locomotive until you see the whole string of cars behind it. If you find losers in the train, take a closer look at the locomotive before you hitch up. The first two years of your association with any organization are the most critical, so take your time in selecting a locomotive, and once you select one, stick with it.

How can you stay close to your locomotive, or "star"? If he or she is in a bowling league, join the team. If your star lives on the north side of town, move there. If your star is a member of a country club, join it. Don't worry about little things like your wife having plenty of clothes, an extra pair of shoes for baby, or building a savings account. All these things will come your way if you hitch your wagon to the right star. If your star has a favorite bar, frequent it. And if your star is photographed, dash to the locale and then casually stand next to him. Should you end up next to the wrong person, find a reason to vacate the premises at once. It's an anathema to be photographed with a loser.

Some people pick more than one locomotive. Then, as they get derailed, they concentrate on the locomotives that are left. This is dangerous, but if you are devious enough it can work. Phil Pockets tried it.

Phil's favorite statement is, "Nobody's going to stick me with one locomotive. I'm part of eight trains going to the top." Phil really believes in the Company Photograph Theory. So much so that three years ago he started carrying one of those tiny pocket cameras wherever he went. Any time a "star" company official was around, he'd work his way over to him and then ask somebody to take his picture. As soon as the film was developed, Phil would send a copy of the picture to the star.

A pocket photo album permitted Phil to whip out a picture of himself and whatever person he wanted to be associated with at the time. If he was with Ivan Kingman, Phil would show Ivan a picture of himself and Ivan's son—with Phil's arm around young Kingman's shoulders, of course. He could do the same with any one of the eight locomotives he was hitched to. But we said this is dangerous. Phil was doing fine until, by some quirk of fate, he ended up standing next to Dee Endd at the company picnic. You see, all eight of his stars were in the picture, so he had to take the empty spot next to Dee. Tough luck, Phil.

While the Company Photograph Theory works well, it takes more time and effort than most people are willing to spend. But it is the fastest way to the top. And it may be the *only* way to one of the top three or four positions in your company. If you opt for this theory, be relentless in your efforts to be photographed with your star. Eat lunch with him. Have coffee breaks with him. Play golf or tennis with him. Associate socially with him. Attend parties with him. In short, dedicate your life to developing a close association with him. You can see why it is so important to pick the right star!

Listen, we're as sorry as you are that the Company Photograph Theory works. But we thought you ought to know. You may not have the time or inclination to use this theory but you should be aware of it. At least you can wave knowingly as each train passes by!

———

Moral:
Every time the camera's clicked,
Be standing near the star you picked.

CALENDAR THEORY

Theory in brief:
Don't make a date with time unless you intend to keep it.

We have the solar year, the lunar year, the Gregorian Calendar, the Julian Calendar, and several other measurements of time. Since the invention of the calendar, leaders of organizations have been playing with it to their own advantage. In recent history, President Franklin Delano Roosevelt changed the date of Thanksgiving; President Lyndon Baines Johnson even had the audacity to move the date of George Washington's birthday. Now that's going some.

But these are nothing compared to the way management and their subordinates play fast and loose with the calendar. Let's eavesdrop on a few conversations in Easy Sales Corp. to see how the calendar comes into play every day:

Denny Dart to Wendy Watch: "Send this letter to Harvey Harpooner, but date it last Friday. That's the day I told him I'd send him the information."

Phil Pockets to Norman New: "Buy exactly $2,310 worth of supplies before December 31. No, Norman, it doesn't matter that we don't need the supplies. If we don't buy them, we'll lose the money from next year's budget."

Ima Stickler to Randy Rightman: "If you don't take your vacation by July 1, you'll lose it."

Tom Tough to Swann Songue: "Our reputation is on the line. You *will* finish the report by February 1 if you have to work around the clock."

You might get the impression from these conversations that the calendar is always the enemy. Not true. You noticed, of course, that Denny Dart back-dated his memo to his own advantage. Denny is a calendar manipulator extraordinaire. Let's watch him in action.

While dropping in his coins and waiting for the coffee to trickle into his cup, Randy casually mentions to a group an idea that he thinks will greatly help Easy Sales Corp. Denny listens with interest. "Good idea," he thinks. After casually strolling out the door, Denny races to his desk and whips off a memo to his supervisor, Tom Tough. You can guess what it said—it's Randy Rightman's idea. "Wendy, this must get out today, and make sure it has today's date on it," Denny screams. I'm sure you understand his logic; it's kind of like a copyright date. By the time Randy works out the details of his idea and presents it to Tom Tough, Denny will have the credit.

The calendar can be used for or against subordinates. We need to understand how it's used in order to turn the tables on the Denny Darts and Tom Toughs of the world. Here are a few uses of the calendar:

Back-dating. If letters or reports are due on a certain day but that date cannot be met, put the due date on the document.

Copyright. History will decide who originated an idea by the date on the first document to deal with the subject. Ask Randy about this one.

Target dates. Look out when your boss casually drops a target date for a project. That date may mean nothing to him when he first mentions it, but, if you accept the date, it will become critical. The time to challenge a target date is when it's first mentioned.

Days off. Some organizations say it's good for everyone to take off the first two weeks of July, so they set those days aside as a factory vacation. The truth is they're the best days for factory maintenance. Some say Good Friday is a holiday; others don't. Some say you must work until quitting time Christmas Eve; others let you party between 3:30 and 5:00 that day. Managers love the feeling of power that they get from arbitrarily setting the holiday schedule for the troops.

Deadlines. Work should never be declared done until it's due. If you turn in work ahead of time, you will be asked to change it. Remember the time Wendy Watch typed thirty-seven individualized letters and gave them to Tom Tough two days early? Tom changed two "critical" words in all thirty-seven letters. Wendy worked overtime to retype them. If she had waited until the deadline, it would have been too late for Tom Tough to insist on an insignificant change.

Anniversary dates. These are most important. All company benefits revolve around these dates. You are hired on your anniversary day, retire on that day, become entitled to your vacation on that day, and receive benefit changes on that day. You are your anniversary date.

Fiscal years. Money and the calendar go together. Today you can spend nothing because it's the end of the old fiscal year and the budget's busted. You must get by on what you have. Work overtime without pay. Use the backs of envelopes. Keep the heat turned down. Don't expect a raise. Tomorrow a new fiscal year begins and that means a new budget. Now you have plenty of money. You can buy supplies. Go to a conference. Work overtime. What a difference a day makes! Twenty-four little hours! It may be hard to comprehend, but it's true.

Now it's plain that the calendar can be a friend or an enemy. Once you understand its importance, you can add it to your growing repertoire of theories to help you manage management.

Moral:
The calendar can be your end,
Or just about your dearest friend.

PAPER AVALANCHE
THEORY

Theory in brief:
A little knowledge raises questions, a lot
is overwhelming; so to overcome your boss's insecurities,
and to keep him off your back, bury him
in an avalanche of paper.

In the day-to-day saga of modern management, the boss often gets in the way of progress. Management's insecurities often show up in their insistence on frequent meetings and interim progress reports. Such meetings and reports serve only to slow you down at the critical points in your project. It's obvious that you need some way to keep the boss informed enough so that he doesn't slow you down. Here is a true-to-life experience that will help you.

Randy Rightman was given the job of developing the

specifications for a new computer system, a job which called for long hours of work if the demanding schedule was to be met. Randy used every minute to best advantage. He consulted with many experts and documented every step he took. Randy was sure that his thoroughgoing approach would please Harvey Harpooner, the controller.

However, from Harpooner's perspective, things didn't look good at all. True, Randy always seemed busy, but he never seemed to have time to talk about the project. Harpooner began to suspect that Randy's preoccupation with the task at hand was due to his having fallen behind schedule. "After all," Harpooner reasoned, "everybody knows that if you just let someone do a job without supervision, he will slack off." So like any "good" manager, Harpooner called Randy on the carpet to berate him for falling behind schedule.

After listening to Harpooner's doubts and innuendos about falling behind on the project, Randy pleaded: "I have been working hard, Mr. Harpooner. The project is even ahead of schedule and I am very pleased with the way things are going." "Randy," Harpooner retorted, "if you had things under control, you would have reported to me about the project. As it is, I just can't be sure that we are going to meet the critical date."

And that was just the beginning. Harpooner continued his harangue for thirty minutes. After this executive pep talk, Randy was distraught. Harpooner could see this, and he was delighted. Randy thought he had been shot down, but Harpooner felt warm inside. He thought, "I've finally got that boy back on the right track."

When he left Harpooner's office, Randy was confused. He knew the project was going well, but, after all, Mr. Harpooner was the controller. Randy concluded that perhaps he should be working harder. So he did. His ten-hour days stretched into twelve-hour days. He interviewed, he wrote, he planned, he devised, he scheduled, he flow-charted, he documented. Whatever could possibly be needed, he did. "Wow!" thought an elated Randy. "This project is going to get me promoted."

Right in the middle of Randy's reverie, Harpooner stormed into his office to demand that Randy get moving on the project. Randy's jaw dropped and he stared in disbelief as a furious Mr. Harpooner stomped out the door.

The next day Randy visited his friend Sam Smoothwater. After he had explained the problem to him, Sam said, "What you have to do, Randy, is learn to manage Harpooner!" "How do I manage the controller?" asked a bewildered Randy. "There are lots of ways," said Sam, "but in this case, the remedy is simple. You have to use diversionary tactics to keep Harpooner off your back until you get the project done. The tactic that will work here is to create a series of paper avalanches at just the right time."

"How do I do that?" moaned Randy. "It's simple," replied Sam. "Tomorrow, get together copies of all the paper work that you have done until now. Send Harpooner copies of your notes from interviews, copies of all documentation you want him to see, copies of your work sheets, copies of statistics you have collected."

"What good will all that do?" said Randy. "Mr. Harpooner doesn't know the first thing about computers *or* the project. I don't see what he will learn from all this or how it will keep him off my back."

"Randy, you've got a lot to learn. Managers like Harpooner become insecure when they feel you haven't taken them into your confidence during the working phase of a project. Like a lot of other so-called modern managers, Harpooner is convinced that his employees won't work unless they are closely supervised. Of course, Harpooner doesn't know enough about what you are doing to really supervise you, so he wants reports. He wants to see quantities of work. That will reassure him that something is happening on the project."

A light began to dawn in Randy's eyes. "You know, you're right, Sam. I can just see Mr. Harpooner going over all those documents. He won't be able to make head or tail of them, but I bet he'll love them."

"No doubt about it," Sam said. "You see, if you slide an avalanche of paper over Harpooner periodically, you will overcome his 'no watch, no work' attitude."

Randy hurried to his office. That night he whistled while he worked. Next morning at 8:30 A.M. he walked into Harpooner's office with his "report." He handed Harpooner a memo covering thirty-five legal-sized sheets just loaded with data. Harpooner smiled broadly and said, "Fine, Randy, fine!" Three days later Randy met Harpooner walking through the general office. Harpooner patted him on the back and said, "Keep up the good work, my boy!"

"So that's how Sam keeps the water so smooth,"

thought Randy. Later that day, after thanking Sam for the advice, Sam explained to him the simple rules of the Paper Avalanche Theory:

Send your boss a copy of all outgoing correspondence. If he doesn't get a copy, he won't believe you did it.

When in doubt, send him a memo. It's much better to send the boss too much than too little.

Send your boss copies of incoming correspondence. If he doesn't know you're being asked to do something, he won't know you did it.

Send your boss copies of work sheets, statistics, reports, whatever—it'll keep him busy. A busy boss is rarely a troublesome boss.

The best way to use the Paper Avalanche Theory is to keep a little paper descending on the boss every day. Then when a critical date approaches, unleash an avalanche of paper on him. Since management gets nervous just prior to critical dates, your avalanche will keep them in their offices shoveling their way out—and off your back.

No doubt you have noticed the avalanche of paper work that falls on everyone involved when a big meeting is about to begin, a start-up date is reached, or the like. This is the Paper Avalanche Theory in action.

A final word of caution. Keep your snow blower poised for action, aimed in the right direction—and watch your timing. Just in case, keep your galoshes handy.

Moral:
When your boss is bugging you
with questions and/or meetings,
Send a paper avalanche
complete with season's greetings.

WALKING ENCYCLOPEDIA THEORY

Theory in brief:
If you present enough statistics,
sooner or later management will believe *you* know
what you are doing even if *they* don't.

Scientific management is in, and seat-of-the-pants management is out. Modern managers use game theory, regression analysis, return on investment, and other scientific methods to reach decisions. Today, most managers believe that the romantic era of gut feelings and manager's intuition is a thing of the past. But it is not as passé as you may have been led to believe.

Many managers are presented an impressive array of statistics when they are about to make a decision. Unfortunately, many of these same managers understand very little of the data at their disposal.

It is for this reason that the Walking Encyclopedia Theory is so effective. This theory states that given the present blind acceptance of "scientific management principles," statistics are irrefutable. Since this is so, to manage management you must present enough statistics to convince management you know what you are doing. Just as one more straw added to a capacity load will break the camel's back, so just one more statistic added to an "irrefutable" statistical argument will break down the resistance of a recalcitrant manager.

To illustrate the point, you are invited to be an observer during a meeting of middle-level managers. They are meeting to reach a decision on whether to computerize a certain segment of operations. Tom Tough was assigned to do the feasibility study. He is pleading his case before these sophisticated, scientific sovereigns of industry.

Tom has one of the prime requisites to make this presentation: confidence. Management likes that. And nothing bolsters confidence better than "facts." Tom knows this and, for this reason, he is a veritable walking encyclopedia.

In selling the idea of a new accounts-receivable system, Tom begins by citing statistics: "Studies have shown that it takes an average clerk seven and one-half minutes to look up information on nonstandard requests. Applying the same methods of study to our unique situation in Easy Sales Corp., we find that our own clerks spend 6 percent more time than the average throughout the industry. We also find that 2.1 invoices out of 40 must be rewritten because certain data are lacking when the invoice is first prepared. Based on these and other statistics—such as the time spent correcting errors, time

124

lost because of improper work flow, and the like—we will be able to use our present staff for the next five years. This is based on the statistics which show that the new system will be 13 percent more efficient in clerical entries, reduce errors by 14.3 percent, and increase productivity by a whopping 16.3 percent. What all this means is that at the end of five years, instead of increasing our labor force by 10 percent, we will keep the same number of employees. Based on an 8.1 percent increase in the cost of living, which would affect salaries, and the possibility of a 20 percent increase in fringe benefit costs, we should realize a 17.5 percent return on investment as compared to a 16 percent increase on investment throughout the industry."

By now the eyes of all the managers present are as wide as saucers. This all sounds just great to them. And no wonder. Tom Tough presents each statistic authoritatively and boldly. Keep in mind that while they may ask an occasional question, they really know very little about the technical trivia that Tom triumphantly presents.

The Walking Encyclopedia Theory requires that some of the statistics be factual. But what makes the theory work is the abundance of nonscientifically collected statistics that surround and gain credence from the valid statistics. The truth is that many of Tom's technical interpretations were conjured up through his crystal ball. Sadly, nonscientific statistics are very easy to find and are just as impressive as the real thing.

Take that return-on-investment percentage Tom threw around for the "industry." When he was asked where he got that one, Tom said, "A team of statisticians from M.I.T. presented this and other statistics at a computer conference I attended." What could the managers say? They could only nod their heads and okay Tom's proposal. Little did they know that Tom's irrefutable statistic was casually dropped after three drinks in the hotel bar.

The great success of the Walking Encyclopedia Theory is due to the fact that statisticians are rarely called upon to prove the validity of their samples. It's the same with you. How often, after reading some statistic or other in a magazine, do you inquire as to how the sample was obtained, what the confidence limits were, and other relevant information? Virtually never, right? The same is true with managers.

If you think we are exaggerating, try this. At your next business meeting, casually drop a statistic into the conversation and observe how ready the group is to accept it. Now try to imagine how much more readily they will accept a statistic you drop into a presentation already buttressed with several valid statistics. You will be amazed.

And if anybody calls you a walking encyclopedia, take it as a compliment. You are on your way to big things.

Moral:
Cite a figure, make it stick.
Lots of stats will turn the trick.

GROUP
3

Theories Designed to Make Management Do It Your Way

TRIAL BALLOON THEORY

Theory in brief:
A weak swimmer who swims with the tide will beat
a strong one who swims against it.

Easy Sales Corporation was looking for a new location for its international headquarters. George Goodman got this prized assignment—a "plum" (see Personal Dow-Jones Theory). George felt that, if he performed well on this assignment, it might be the turning point in his career. From a relatively obscure position, George would be brought into direct contact with the top officials of his corporation. He would no longer be old what's-his-name but would be George Goodman, a successful, hard-working, ingenious member of the team.

In keeping with the magnitude of the assignment, George was thorough. He studied the cost of real estate, the tax structures of various communities, the employment picture, prevailing wage scales in each area, and much more.

George made comparative studies of predicted wage and tax rates over the next ten to twenty-five years and worked up detailed reports on thirteen other factors that lesser men would not even have considered.

Then, based on a scientifically developed algorithm, George had all these facts run through the computer. The indisputable results showed that corporate headquarters should be moved from downtown New York City to Bergen County, New Jersey.

George was bursting with enthusiasm. He couldn't wait to call a meeting with top management and present to them the results of many weeks, and weekends, of work. When the big day came, George reviewed his findings with top management. Fact after fact was presented with graphs, charts, and other visual displays. The benefits of moving to Bergen County were forcefully explained.

What was the result? How did management react to George's thoroughgoing, objective search for truth? They promoted him to a seat on the board, right? Wrong! Management shot holes in his reports. They wondered out loud how George could have come up with such an illogical choice as Bergen County, New Jersey.

Where did George go wrong? Did he fail to consider all the factors? Yes. George neglected to find out which way the tide was running. Our hard-working, ingenious, would-be member of the team made a fatal mistake. He went "against the tide."

George made the common mistake of taking management at its word, of thinking that what management wanted was a thorough analysis of the facts and a logical decision based on those facts. George failed to realize that what management wanted was to have its biased, illogical decision supported. Had George kown what management wanted, and recommended what management wanted, he would have become that successful member of the team he wished to be.

How could George have found out what management wanted? How does the weatherman find out which way the wind is blowing? He releases a trial balloon. How does a golfer check the wind before his shot? He pulls up a few blades of grass and throws them into the air. Another trial balloon. If a swimmer wants to make time and save energy, what does she do? She swims with the tide.

At Easy Sales Corporation the flow of the tide was so great that even the strongest swimmer would have lost ground swimming against it. Subordinates like George need to learn this lesson quickly or they will find themselves sucked under the surface by undercurrents they do not even suspect exist.

Let's assume that George now realizes that he cannot successfully swim against the tide. How can he use this knowledge to his benefit?

If George had awakened to this fact before starting on his "plum" of an assignment, he could have used the Trial Balloon Theory, which helps a subordinate to avoid swimming against the tide of management's river of opinions. To wit:

> If you release an idea as a trial balloon and it is shot down, don't be too quick to stick out your neck;

OR

Only a damned fool would make a recommendation
that has already been rejected.

This is not to say that trial balloons that have been shot
down or paper ships that have been sunk always spell doom
for ideas. It is possible to put across unpopular ideas. But this
requires use of the Turn the Herd Theory (discussed earlier in
the book).

In this case, we'll assume that George was aware of
how difficult it is to go against management's opinion but ig-
norant of the Turn the Herd Theory. What should he have
done?

George needed to begin his report by writing its conclusion. The conclusion was easy to surmise in the case of
Easy Sales Corporation. Most of the homes of top management were located in Stamford, Connecticut. George should
have known that. Didn't the top managers always have those
interesting little stories to tell about commuting? Didn't they
continually gripe about having to commute? Where was
George?

Had George put his knowledge of the Trial Balloon
Theory to work, he would have tested the water. He would
have sent up his Stamford balloon to see who would take a
shot at it. If a couple of Stamford balloons survived the flight
or a couple of paper ships made the trip with the tide to Connecticut, then George would already have had his conclusion.

And the fact is that any conclusion that would locate
international headquarters in Stamford, Connecticut, would
have been hailed by the board of directors as the epitome of

wisdom. George could have developed his algorithm around the factors that would have situated headquarters in Stamford.

George would have known that any suggestion of moving headquarters farther away from the hometown of the executives would only increase their commuting time, create problems for the kids in school, break up their wives' bridge groups, and cause numerous other corporate disasters.

Facts, after all, can be used to support many conclusions, but to be implemented, conclusions must be supported by management. The safest course is to test the water and draw the conclusion that goes along with the tide. You will stay afloat much longer.

Here is what we learn from the trial balloon theory:

—If you want to make progress, make sure which way the tide is going before you start swimming. Then swim with it.

—While swimming against the tide is not always fatal, it always creates hardships and retards your progress.

—If the tide is weak, consider using the Turn the Herd Theory to turn the tide.

Moral:

**If your present project has you in confusion,
start off right by noting the conclusion.**

GIMME THEORY

OR

How to Be Sure Everybody Wins

Theory in brief:
Nobody expects *two* Trojan horses!

Perry's Other Perfect Principle
You can get your entire proposal approved by
management
if you have the guts to include a
deliberate flaw for the boss to remove.
Perry's Parallel Precautionary Principle ("Gimme")
Never overestimate the
boss's ability to find a problem—make it obvious.

The Gimme Theory is the original "everybody wins" theory. It is perhaps the easiest one to use, is extremely effective, and provides untold pleasure to management. This theory is based

135

on the fact that most managers manage by challenging the ideas of their subordinates.

It has been said that most people have no more than five truly creative ideas in a lifetime. Since managers are generally appointed after years of experience, it is sad but true that most managers have a zero balance in their creative-ideas bank. Thus they are forced to manage by selecting among the ideas of others. Many are now satisfied with creative negativity. This is manifested by their eagerness to reject ideas.

Before you can effectively implement this theory, you must find out the manager's "negativity quotient."

It's really a matter of fishing with the right bait. Some fish bite on worms, others on dough balls. Which bait is your boss most likely to take? Find out and include it in your proposal deliberately. When your boss bites the bait out of your proposal, you will gain his approval with your real proposal intact.

You'll find the use of the Gimme Theory very rewarding. How happy your boss will be to tear out the vulnerable underbelly of your proposal! And how happy you will be to have him do it!

Inexperienced subordinates tremble at the thought of the boss's finding flaws in their proposals and the prospect of the manager sending them back to the drawing board. If you have planted the flaw (gimme) the boss has harvested, you won't mind, since you will be coming off victorious—a true manager of management.

Lest you cringe at such a "devious" ploy, remember that your boss believes it is his duty to find a flaw. And he will find it, real or imagined. By planting the flaw, you are helping your inept manager to carry out his duty properly. Left to himself, he may decide that some vital area of your proposal is the flaw.

You are also saving your manager from an ulcer by using the Gimme Theory. How, you ask? Have you any idea how frustrated managers become when they encounter a perfect proposal? Generally, they become so frustrated that they reject it altogether. This is based on the manager's inalienable right to reject coupled with his innate fear of the hidden flaw.

Here are some fake flaws (gimmes) that make very effective bait:

Cost cutting. Since the boss likes to slash dollars, add a dollar figure that he can cut out without hurting your project (for details, see Double Cut Theory).

Word changing. The boss just loves to change the way things are said. Use some wording your boss is sure to hate.

Frill cutting. The boss takes pride in "getting it down to essentials." Add a frill he can refuse (see Glass House Theory).

Responsibility moving. The boss thinks he can pick the right person to do the job. Pick the wrong person. When he corrects you, you will have the right person. (If he doesn't realize you picked the wrong person, you can change it later.)

Schedule changing. The boss always wants to see things done more quickly. Add extra time for him to cut down (see Man on the Moon Theory).

And here is a Peter Piper illustration of the Gimme Theory: Penny Push penciled a pretty proposal for a project. Peter Planner promptly prophesied a problem. "Please, Peter," Penny panted, "pick a ploy to put in my proposal." Peter pictured the president poking the proposal for a problem. Plenty of problems could be planted in the proposal. "Plant a phony problem in the proposal," Penny panted. Peter planted. Penny's purpose in planting the problem was to permit the president to promptly pick the problem and present it to her. Penny Push would then praise the president for precociously perceiving a potential problem. Pres would then permit Penny to perform the project. This preposterous personification puts the ploy in the proper perspective.

A word of caution. Penny put the problem in the proper place—where it couldn't be missed. Don't overestimate your boss's ability to find a problem. Place the problem in the most obvious spot, let the boss find it, and when he does, say, "Good find, boss." The net result is that the boss feels he is smarter than you and you have gotten what you wanted. That's why the Gimme Theory could also be called the "everybody wins" theory.

Moral:
Proposals perfect cause a glitch
In presidents and bosses.
So leave a flaw that they can find,
Which very little loss is.

ATOM BOMB
THEORY

**Theory in brief:
If you want to drop a big bomb,
see a big boss.**

During World War II the United States Air Force routinely dropped thousands of bombs on Japanese territory. Any lieutenant on an atoll in the Pacific could order bomb raids that could, over a period of time, destroy entire cities. Such decisions drew little attention from the handful of people who were running the war.

On July 16, 1945, the first atomic bomb was exploded near Alamogordo, New Mexico, with a force equal to 17,000 tons of TNT. While many a lieutenant ordered the dropping of bombs with a total explosive force of well over 17,000 tons of TNT, it took a decision by the Commander in Chief of all the armed forces of the United States to drop *one bomb* with the explosive force of 17,000 tons of TNT. Why?

Because ordering bombing raids with smaller payloads was routine regardless of the total explosive force. Dropping one such powerful bomb was not routine. This fact teaches us an important lesson about managing management: if you want a positive decision, you must seek the proper level of management to consider the proposition. For instance, what would have happened if a lieutenant on a Pacific atoll had been confronted with the decision to drop or not to drop the atomic bomb? He would have said, "I am only authorized to drop bombs with the explosive force of up to fifty tons of TNT. I can't make the decision." And the decision would be successively passed up the line until someone was authorized to make it. In this case it turned out to be Harry S. Truman.

It's the same in business. If you take a proposal to your manager for approval, it must fall within his realm of authority and it must also be something he is used to handling. Otherwise, he will reject the proposal no matter how good it is. Let's look at an example.

Sam Smoothwater wants two new office chairs. Mary Mouth authorizes furniture purchases up to $300. Sam knows very well that Mary will not authorize any furniture for him, yet what he wants will cost $250—and that is within Mary's approval limit. What will Sam do?

Since Sam is smart, he uses the Atom Bomb Theory. He asks for the two chairs—as well as a corner table, a new desk, and a bookcase. When the request lands on Mary Mouth's desk, the total cost of the requisition is $985. Mary wishes she could shoot down Sam's proposal, but it is way above her approval limit, so she passes it up to Randy Rightman who, Sam knows, is in favor of upgrading the company's image. Result: Sam is now sitting in his office enjoying his new furniture.

Here's another example. Suppose you knew that your company desperately needed an online data processing system. You work up a proposal and find that you can install an adequate system for $850,000. In Easy Sales Corp., Harvey Harpooner, your controller, approves proposals over $500,000 but less than $1,000,000. If you send your proposal to him, you know it will be rejected. Should you doom a good project to failure by sending it to Harpooner? Not on your tape drive!

You know the Atom Bomb Theory. Use it! You refigure your proposal, adding some of the extras you had cut out. The total now comes to $1,200,000. While the additional $350,000 isn't essential, it can be used profitably to upgrade the hardware and provide for future growth. Your proposal still has to go to Harvey Harpooner, but when he sees the total cost, he will send the proposal to the President and Chairman of the Board, Ivan Kingman. That's what you wanted. You know that Kingman is pro-computer. Harpooner, who is anti-computer, can't do a thing to stop you. It's in Ivan's hands now! The Atom Bomb Theory works again. You and your company gain. In the unlikely event that you don't need the extra $350,000, you can return it to the company's coffers and become a local hero for bringing the project in under budget.

So, when you are about to make a proposal, think atom bomb. Upgrade your firecracker to a good-sized bomb to get the attention of the approval-level manager. Remember, it's easy for your immediate superior to reject a low-budget idea, but virtually impossible for him to stop an idea involving big money. In other words, it may be easier to get a yacht than a row boat. It may be easier to build a new building than to expand an old one. Think big! Big enough to reach the level of management at which you have a good chance of a favorable decision.

Moral:
If just one thing will get a yes,
The atom bomb would be the best.

THE HAMMER
THEORY

Theory in brief:
Give a kid a hammer and he'll pound
everything in sight.

Once upon a time, there was a little boy named Ivan King-man. Ivan lived in a house nestled in a shady lot on Sleepy Hollow Cove. Ivan's house was new and shiny. The walls were solid and the doors were tight. The floors were all sturdily constructed by expert craftsmen.

On Ivan's seventh birthday his loving parents gave him a hammer. What a happy day it was for little Ivan. It didn't take him long to figure out how to use his new present. And what diverse uses he found for it. Little Ivan tightened all the nails in the floor. He banged the door hinges down tight. He carefully hammered the dowels in each chair so that they were extra snug. He even saw to it that the walls were attached more securely by banging strategic and not-so-strategic spots. Yes, Ivan found everything in the house that needed pounding and then some.

On his seventeenth birthday, Ivan had a little car. It's paint was white as snow. And everywhere that Ivan went, the car was sure to go. Ivan couldn't walk half a block anymore. He had to use the car. Then, Ivan got a job at Easy Sales Corp. He was given a dictating machine. From that moment on every utterance that Ivan made was recorded. He even dictated his checks! Ivan would not even initial time cards. Instead he dictated his initials! Yes, Ivan was an instrument addict—and as President of Easy Sales Corp., he still is.

What can you learn from Ivan? It's this: if you give a child a hammer, he will pound everything in sight. The hammer is symbolic of many managerial toys. Put a toy in the hands of a manager and he will find 101 ways to use it.

This overuse of managerial toys can be explained in two ways. First, the fascination of a new toy compels its owner to play with it constantly. Second, the toy evokes jealousy in others—once they see it they want it. In industry, we call these toys status symbols.

Let's look at a few corporate toys. The training department is given closed-circuit TV equipment. They immediately find oodles of ways to use it. All corporate training should be televised and played back. Transactional analysis is added to the training program—stressing role playing. Why? It's good TV fare. All seminars must include a TV segment. Employee orientation is televised and played to each new member.

If a mechanic is given a new piece of test apparatus, he

will use it to check out every problem—even if he knows exactly what the problem is without testing. If the president of the company goes to a seminar and learns about calculating return on investment, he will make every business decision based on that theory. And everyone else will have to use that method too. If the company guard is given a sign-in log, he will make everyone sign it every time they pass through the portals of Easy Sales Corp. We love our corporate toys and use them every chance we get.

Here is a list of executive hammers:

Computers. This is the number-one hammer for all managers, who will use the computer for every process in the organization. The programmer will computerize the company bowling team scores and those of their competitors. Around December 25th, computer services will print out pictures of Santa and Rudolph. Managers have even tried, unsuccessfully, to use the computer to replace clerks.

Mergers. For a time, this hammer pounded little companies into big ones. While mergers are losing their popularity, they were used and abused for some time.

Benefit plans. Executives really took to this one. They added benefits galore: better pension plans, better dental health-care plans, beefed-up tuition aid plans. Now they are finding they have more plans than money.

Technology. Improved technical apparatus is the high priestess of all organizations. Executives hooked on this hammer believe that technology is the panacea for all ills.

Job rotation. Managers decided the best way to train people
was to move them around. The I've Been Moved Company (IBMCO) thought they might be overdoing it
when their second largest expense item turned out to
be MOVING EXPENSES.

The unbridled use of the Hammer Theory can work to
the disadvantage of subordinates, to say nothing of the company. However, if you know the theory well you can avert disaster. For instance, Ivan Kingman attended an executive
training session at a well-known university a few months ago.
During the meetings, he learned the secretarial pool concept
and how many secretaries can be replaced by using it. Upon
returning from the campus, Ivan and his three vice presidents
met to organize an executive secretarial pool.

Sam Smoothwater saw the handwriting on the wall. He
knew that Ivan had a new toy. He also knew that Ivan would
find ways to use it even where it wouldn't work. And Sam
realized that it was only a matter of time until his faithful secretary, Wendy Watch, would be taken from him and thrown
into the pool.

Sam sprang into action. He began to say that he no
longer needed a secretary. "What I need," said Sam, "is an
administrative assistant." With that, Sam rewrote Wendy's
job description, had it duly approved and filed. Of course, this
had no effect whatever on what Wendy did. She just had a
new title.

As Sam expected, Ivan strode through the offices one
day and saw something which threw him into a rage. All his
subordinates had private secretaries. "This will never do,"

proclaimed Ivan, "I'll establish a secretarial pool for subordinates." And he did. Of course, Sam wasn't worried. Wendy was an administrative assistant. When the secretaries were thrown into the pool, Wendy was high and dry just outside Sam's office.

Within two months after returning from the seminar with his new toy, Ivan had played with it in every department of Easy Sales Corp. Only Sam Smoothwater, who understood the Hammer Theory, saved his secretary from the plunge.

On the other hand, let's suppose that Sam did not have a secretary or administrative assistant. Suppose further that he needed one, but the Glass House Theory had him stymied. Sam could have urged Ivan Kingman to play with his new secretarial pool toy. Once the pool was installed, Sam would have access to secretarial help he couldn't get any other way. Would Sam go so far as to suggest that Ivan attend a seminar promoting the secretarial pool concept? If that was the only way to get the help he needed, why not!

As you can see, the Hammer Theory works both ways. And this is one candle you can burn at both ends.

Moral:
If your boss has got a toy,
Use the Hammer Theory ploy.

NEGATIVE-POSITIVE THEORY

Theory in brief:
Management will make you do what they think
you don't want to do. So let them.

Of all the theories in this book, this is the only one that's un-ethical. You will probably want to skip the Positive-Negative Theory because, if you read it, you may be tempted to use it on your boss to your own advantage. Since I am sure you would not want to use something less than totally ethical on your boss, I suggest you stop reading here and go on to the next theory.

Since you are reading this sentence, you have proved the allure of the Positive-Negative Theory. Once we find something we shouldn't do, are told not to do, or are warned that doing it may lead to some evil consequence, we are sure to entertain doing it.

The essence of the Negative-Positive Theory is that when you want someone to do something, tell him not to do it.

Why is it that people cannot resist reacting positively to the negative? It's easy to explain. There are two parts to the Positive-Negative Theory. First there's a temptation, then there's the challenge. You tempt your subject when you make him or her aware of a proscribed condition or thing. You issue the challenge when you say, "Whatever you do, don't give in to this temptation!"

These elements are summed up in the gift card which says DON'T OPEN UNTIL CHRISTMAS. You may wait until Christmas Eve, but never until Christmas.

Parents who don't understand this theory drive their children into temptation and sin. Take li'l Harvey Harpooner's mother, for example. It's the day before Halloween and Mother says to nine-year-old Harvey, "The candy in the buffet is for Halloween." Up until now Harvey wasn't tempted by the candy; he didn't even know it was in the house. His mother has succeeded in placing an irresistible temptation in front of him. Now comes the challenge. "And, young man," she says, "don't you dare eat one bite of that candy until after tomorrow night." Can any red-blooded American boy resist a challenge like that? Of course not. Harvey succumbs and gorges himself. Don't blame Harvey; he didn't have a chance. Put the blame on ignorance—ignorance of the Negative-Positive Theory. But, dear reader, from Harvey's sad experience you can learn how to get people to do things they don't want to do. Just tell them *not* to do it and, sure enough, they will.

Managers can't resist the negative-positive treatment any more than little Harvey Harpooner could. Big Harvey can be manipulated just as easily by the negative-positive. Why, only yesterday Wendy Watch sauntered into Harvey's office at 11:25 and said, "Mr. Harpooner, I probably shouldn't go to Sally's luncheon with the other girls at 11:30, don't you agree?" Harvey likes to say no, so he accepts this challenge and says, "No, I don't agree. You go right along with the others." "Oh, thank you, Mr. Harpooner," says Wendy, and joins the other girls waiting for her downstairs.

To get the most out of your manager with the Negative-Positive Theory, you need a thorough understanding of the eleven motivators that work best. The one that moved Harvey Harpooner to let Wendy go to lunch early was the leadership motivator. Let's look at all eleven:

Leadership motivator. When you use this motivator, you imply that if your boss fails to go along with what you ask, he lacks leadership ability, since all the other company leaders are doing it. For example, you might make a statement such as, "I'll bet you wouldn't let me do what Ivan Kingman and Phil Pockets are letting their people do, would you?" That type of question is a surefire motivator for those in leadership positions.

Sex motivator. Hang your appeal on favorable traits associated with a person's sex. For example, a man is supposed to be strong, right? So Sally Single says, "I was going to ask you to help me move my desk, but you might hurt yourself." That statement will make a man throw away his truss and move a mountain.

Position motivator. Appeal to the authority that goes with a person's position. For example, say, "Can you approve this, or must I take it to someone higher up?" If it is humanly possible, you will get the approval you seek.

Pride motivator. When someone takes pride in his achievements and is ambitious, this motivator will work. Say something like, "I was going to ask you to handle this project for me, but I don't know if you've ever worked on something this complex." Your manager's pride will make him accept the challenge.

Straight-shooter motivator. People who pride themselves on doing the right thing—being straight shooters—cannot resist a statement like, "It sure would be nice to send flowers to Will Workman, but I don't think we can bend company policy to do that, do you?" Just watch policy bend!

Greed motivator. If your boss is the type who's always looking out for number one, he'll almost always bite on a statement like, "Sam said we need four more chairs in our office, but I was thinking maybe we ought to wait until Mr. Harpooner gets all his equipment, don't you?" Your boss will probably hiss through gritted teeth, "Get those chairs in here tomorrow!"

Hate motivator. Hate tends to eat people up inside, and they don't think too clearly. So if you know your boss dislikes another person, you can turn his hate to positive

154

action. Say, "I don't think we ought to proceed with Project A, it might make Denny Dart look bad." Chances are your boss will assign top priority to *anything* that will make Denny look bad. If it doesn't make Denny look bad, so what? Is your boss going to go around screaming, "We completed Project A and it didn't make Denny look bad"?

Justice motivator. If your boss claims to be the epitome of justice, he'll dance to your tune if you say, "Even if Will Workman did work during Thanksgiving and Christmas holidays, why should we give him time off for his kid's graduation?"

Revenge motivator. Admittedly, this is base. But why not try to get good out of evil? Let's say Denny Dart has done something mean to your boss, but you know that Denny's wife is sick and Denny needs money. You could say, "Boss, I sure hope poor Denny doesn't have to work late this week, he needs the time off." Count on it, your vengeful boss will make Denny work overtime. Boss will be happy, and Denny will ransom his wife from the hospital.

Competition motivator. This is the greatest motivator in the business world. If you let your boss know that a rival department might be doing something that will move them up a notch in the pecking order, you'll get what you want. How about this: "Remember I was talking to you about that training trip to Hawaii? Well, I don't think I need to go now. I hear that Sam Smoothwater from the payroll department is going, and he can bring back the tips on how to improve our cash flow." Your boss's competitive spirit will move him to send you to Hawaii over your loudest protests.

Cheapskate motivator. If your boss hates to spend money, even that can be helpful at times. For example, if you don't want to take a trip, you might say, "I am really looking forward to this trip, but it's going to cost a bundle." Old Cheapskate will be glad to have you stay home, and your wife will be pleased to have you home for your twenty-fifth wedding anniversary.

If you are positive you want something, be negative to your boss. Decide which motivator will work best, and motivate your boss to do what you want him to by telling him not to do it. More than likely, he'll accept the challenge.

Oh, what if the motivator you choose doesn't work? You know the old saying, If at first you don't succeed, try, try again!

Moral:
If you really want it, tell your boss you don't
'Cause if he thinks you do, it's sure as hell he won't.

POCKET VETO
THEORY

Theory in brief:
If your boss says "I'll think about it," your
suggestion is probably vetoed.

The most powerful of all management tools is the pocket veto. It is used by all levels of management right up to the President of the United States. The theory is used by managers to avoid that most dreaded act—making a decision. As a subordinate, you must not forget that decisions terrify managers because any decision can be wrong. Managers never want to be wrong.

Pocket vetoes are devices used to avoid making decisions. This accounts for their popularity. The use of this theory is simple. The manager just puts the request for a decision in a "pocket" and leaves it there until the subordinate forgets about it or gives up. Management has several names for these pockets—in-baskets, tickler files, suspense files, action files, and bottom drawers.

Here are the simple steps in a pocket veto:

1—The subordinate requests that the manager make a decision.
2—The manager asks the subordinate to write up his problem with recommendations for its solution. (This dodge alone is estimated to eliminate three out of five decisions.)
3—The subordinate gives the manager a write-up complete with recommendations.
4—The manager places the write-up in a "pocket" and that is the last anyone ever hears of it.

Penny Push ran into the pocket veto several weeks ago, but she doesn't know it yet. She had been spending a lot of time painfully waiting in line for the restroom. She also noted that Easy Sales Corp.'s employees were about two-thirds female and one-third male. It didn't take higher mathematics to find out that the men had as many restrooms as the women. "Discrimination," thought Penny. "These chauvinistic men have as many restrooms as we do, and in addition to the stall, they even have a urinal. I won't stand for this! What we need in Easy Sales Corp. are unisex restrooms!"

Penny approached her supervisor, Tom Tough, with this idea. "Tom," she said, "I'm sick and tired of waiting in line to use the restroom. Not only is it bad for my health, it's downright discriminatory! Tom, we need to switch our restrooms from sexist to nonsexist. We need unisex restrooms!"

Tom, typical manager that he was, replied, "Very interesting, Penny. I'll need to think about that." As Penny started to walk away, Tom said, "Oh, by the way, Penny, would you write up a memo on the problem and give some details on how we might go about solving it." Penny thought she had already told him, but this seemed to be progress of sorts, so she agreed.

Penny conscientiously prepared the memo as Tom had instructed and gave it to him. "Thanks a lot, Penny," said Tom, carefully placing the memo in his in-basket. When Penny left, Tom stuck the memo at the bottom of the four inches of paper already in the basket.

Penny felt she had accomplished something by getting her suggestion "under management's consideration." Little did she know that once an idea is in a "pocket veto" storage area, it will take an act of Congress to get it out.

You must understand two things about the pocket veto. First, it is extremely powerful and its use widespread. The boss will usually tip his hand as to whether your idea has been vetoed with statements like:

—"I need to think about that."
—"I'll get to it just as soon as possible."
—"I'll have to discuss this with Harvey Harpooner and Ivan Kingman."
—"That is a very interesting idea."

The other thing you need to know about pocket vetoes—and this is most important—is how to get suggestions out of pockets.

Unpocketing maneuvers by subordinates are accepted by management if not practiced too frequently. After all, managers need to unpocket suggestions from higher levels of management. So when a subordinate unpockets an idea from their pocket vetoes, it shows the managers how to get *their* suggestions unvetoed by their bosses.

While unpocketing will not always get the result you want, it *will* cause a decision to be made. To get the right decision, you will probably have to couple unpocketing with some of the other management theories found in this book.

Here are five successful unpocketing techniques listed in order of their known success—the best first:

Carbon copy. When you send your suggestion to the boss, send a copy to *his* boss or someone with a vested interest in your idea. For example, if Penny Push had sent a copy to Mary Mouth, Mary's mouth might have made Tom Tough unpocket the suggestion.

Public issue. At department staff meetings, you can raise your question to your manager in front of all his subordinates. It helps if you get all the support you can before the meeting. Now, if Penny Push had raised the uni-sex-restroom suggestion at a staff meeting, Tom Tough would have been pressured into making a decision. Pocket vetoes are more difficult for managers to pull off when two or more subordinates are involved.

Creeping commitment. If you find that an idea has been pocket-vetoed, it probably was too big a decision for the manager to make. Big decisions are traumatic for managers. Go back with a small part of your suggestion, and get a commitment for that. For example, after two months have passed, Penny will probably realize that her decision has been vetoed. She could ask Tom Tough to designate the men's and women's restrooms in the reception area as simply "Restrooms" so that visitors of either sex could use whichever was available. This is a small decision which Tom will be glad to make. Penny gets one more restroom for her sex, and she has kept Tom from stalling.

The rider. If your suggestion is pocket-vetoed, add it onto something you know the boss wants. In this way, your rider makes a package that the boss won't refuse. The U.S. Congress has used this concept for almost two hundred years with considerable success. If the President vetoes a bill, an enterprising congressperson will add that bill as a rider on another bill that the President wants passed. This puts the President on the horns of a dilemma: if he kills the bill because of the rider, he loses what he wants. He'll generally pass the entire package.

Suggestion box. Most large organizations have a formalized suggestion system. And all suggestions received must be answered. This is especially true in unionized organizations. Although more than 90 percent of all the suggestions received are rejected, you can consider this system as a trial balloon for your idea. Who knows, it may fly! And if it doesn't, you'll find out why. This will give you ammunition for the next battle in your private war.

Business is a game of pocketing and unpocketing vetoes. Since managers always fight savagely for the status quo, any attempt to change things will stand a good chance of being pocket-vetoed. Be alert. Learn how to remove your suggestions from your superior's pockets. It may be pickpocketing, but it's profitable.

Moral:
When your idea's been stuck into a pocket,
Use this theory to get it placed on the docket.

SHOW AND TELL
THEORY

Theory in brief:
To give the business world an enema,
insert the tube in a staff meeting.

In 4003 B.C., Hilkiah Staff organized a spear-making business. Hilkiah's nation was nomadic at the time, and the spear business was sailing along. In just a few months Hilkiah hired an employee to search for stones which would serve for spear heads. Hilkiah was a typical manager. He didn't trust anybody. So he met periodically with his employee to discuss what he had done since the last meeting. Since Elmer Employee was the first subordinate, these meetings were called Hilkiah Staff meetings. In 4001 B.C. this was shortened to "staff" meetings.

We have called meetings between management and subordinates "staff meetings" ever since. This little-known date in history—4003 B.C.—should be remembered for two significant reasons: the first staff meeting occurred at that time, and coincidentally Elmer Employee became the first person to dread staff meetings. He was the forerunner of all the poor subordinates who dread modern-day staff meetings.

The staff meeting may be the oldest of corporate rituals. Certainly it is the most painful. Being fired is only a close second. Today managers call staff meetings for many reasons. High on the list are (1) getting you to do something you don't want to do, and (2) telling you that management doesn't like what you have already done. For instance, at one meeting your sales quota may be raised (to lower your commissions), and at another you may be reprimanded before all onlookers for failing to make your sales quota (which was unreasonably high).

There are four basic types of staff meetings:

Managerial lecture. At this meeting the manager does all the talking. He tells you what you did that was wrong, or he demands that you do things you don't want to do. The manager's lecture is delivered in terms suited to an audience with a two-year-old's mentality. To be sure you don't miss the point, the manager repeats his message two or three times.

Show and tell. At this type of meeting, the manager assembles the troops and asks them, one by one, to show and tell what they have done since the last staff meeting. Experienced subordinates attend this meeting with a variety of visual aids and handouts. One brings a chart, another the latest report, publication, survey, or what-have-you. Others pass out handsomely bound reports of several pages and start their presentation with, "As you can see from this report . . ." when nobody can see anything from that report. Never mind, managers love show and tell.

The critique. During this discouraging meeting, the boss asks various subordinates specific questions or has them explain some project. When the subordinate finishes his or her explanation, the boss gives the "right" answer or explains how the subordinate could have handled the project better. These sessions could also be called the "hindsight meetings." Bosses love them, because bosses always turn out to have 20-20 vision during such sessions.

The combination. The most devastating of all staff meetings, this one begins with the traditional show-and-tell approach, proceeds to the critique phase, and winds up with the grand finale management lecture. The aftereffects of this meeting are almost always the same: nausea, headache, and severe depression on the part of everybody but the one who called it.

In time, all subordinates come to dread the staff meeting. The last time a staff meeting brought good news was in

1901 when Henry Ford announced that his workers' wages would be raised to $2.10 a day. Shortly thereafter Woodrow Wilson initiated the national income tax. That too was announced at a staff meeting.

Even staff meetings can be used to manage management, but we'll get to that later. Right now, let's discuss ways to avoid these dreaded meetings. Here is where good old-fashioned American ingenuity surfaces. Study the following staff meeting dodges carefully; they'll come in handy:

Judicious use of annual leave. Will Workman has twenty days annual leave. He will use at least ten of them in twenty half-day increments on Friday mornings. You guessed it; his staff meetings are on Friday mornings.

Tell the boss I'm sick. Penny Push's female disorders coincide with staff meetings. Since the boss is no gynecologist, what can he say? Anyone who is already out sick will not come back on staff meeting day, and anyone who feels the least bit sick will leave before the staff meeting starts.

Transportation problem ploy. Ken Census always has a flat tire on the morning of the staff meeting. He even had an accident one morning. That was overdoing it.

Hiding in the bushes. (Not recommended).

Travel schedule dodge. This one really works. Randy Rightman schedules all his out-of-town travels to coincide with staff meetings.

Ask for a demotion. This is an extreme method of avoiding

staff meetings. But it has merit. Peace of mind and mental health are worth more than money.

Let's look in on a typical Easy Sales Corp. staff meeting, which Ivan Kingman has decreed all employees will attend, dead or alive. Ivan opens the sullen gathering by asking, "Where's Will Workman?" Wendy meekly murmurs, "He's on the phone about to close a big deal." Ivan proceeds to condemn Will and to give a five-minute lecture on why everyone should be there when Ivan says they should be there. He'll repeat the lecture when Will arrives after closing the big deal. Jay Jokester attempts to lighten the mood by asking if the new dental health plan has any teeth in it. Ivan's icy stare restores the meeting to the proper depth of despondency.

It is show-and-tell time. Ivan growls, "Why don't you start today, Mary Mouth?" Mary explains how Scotch tape usage is up three rolls and that she doesn't know where it is all going. This is Ivan's cue to deliver a seventeen-minute lecture on pilferage and proper use of supplies. "If there is nothing else, how about your report, Tom Tough?" Tom's report is barked out with military precision. "All personnel in my unit arrived at work on time, ate lunch within the one-hour limit, and stayed until after the closing bell, sir." "Good work, Tom," says Ivan, admonishing the rest to follow Tom's good example.

Swann Songue explains how Larry Newbroom helped increase production 184 percent by installing some new improved procedures even though it required him to work several evenings. Ivan quickly retorts that one of Swann's employees was seen arriving at the office three minutes late last week. "You could take a leaf from Tom Tough's book," says Ivan to Swann.

Denny Dart is next. Denny deftly describes how all delays and foul-ups in his department were due to lack of cooperation from other departments. Swann Songue was taken to task again for doing his own work instead of helping Denny. So it goes until finally it is Phil Pockets' turn.

"You're last today, Phil," snorts Ivan. "What's new in your department?" Phil proudly holds up an impressively bound report and says, "See my report. My report is red. The red report says I made a sale. The sale is good. The sale was to a customer. The customer is good. The customer's name is Spender. Let's be nice to Spender." Phil's report made Ivan's day. He beamed as he said, "Good work, Phil. I like your red report."

Now comes the finale. Ivan's tone indicates that what is to follow is confidential. Unfortunately, confidential news from management is always bad news. And the bad news is always blamed on subordinates, who are then charged with the responsibility of remedying the situation. Watch this ploy.

Ivan uses his lowest, most confidential tone, saying, "We've got budgetary problems. We've got to watch every penny we spend. I want you to get the lowest prices on supplies. But don't buy in quantity. I want your staffs to work longer and harder than ever. But no overtime is allowed. And, finally, I want each of you to come up with new and innovative ideas. But keep implementation costs to a bare minimum.

And, by the way, I want more sales with fewer sales calls and less travel expense. That's it for today."

After that little request for the impossible, Ivan's top-level managers are ready to cut their throats. They recognize this speech for what it is: Ivan's reverse Robin Hood plan (taking from the poor and giving to the rich). They all know that the cash flow pinch was caused by investing several million dollars in relocating the home office within two miles of Ivan's palatial residence.

With Ivan's impossible dream ringing in their ears, the employees head back to their work stations, where each one will partake of his or her favorite remedy for staff-meeting blues. This is a critical period for all who attended the meeting. Their thoughts run the gamut of emotions: quitting, punching Ivan in the nose, kicking a hole in their desks, or the peace and quiet of suicide. Some look to lunch and two martinis to get back in the mood to work again. But an hour or two after the meeting, most of the sinking, churning feeling in their stomachs will be gone.

Since you will inevitably face staff meetings in the future, you must learn how to cope with them. Your goal should be to leave a staff meeting in reasonably good health and with your sanity intact. There are eight ways of doing this:

Never argue with the manager. In group situations, the manager must appear to be the boss. Only in one-on-one situations can the boss change his mind and save face.
Prearrange an early exit. This is easily accomplished through an emergency phone call or a visit from your secretary,

who can say that you are desperately needed to handle something you know the boss wants done. The trauma of a staff meeting is proportionate to its length.

Fantasize. By dreaming up happy events or planning your next vacation, you will be able to ignore the proceedings of the meeting. This worked during World War II in the prison camps—an apt analogy.

Write letters. You have no friends at this meeting. Why not keep up your correspondence with those who love you while you listen to those who hate you. Besides, your boss will be impressed. He'll think you are taking notes.

Don't participate. No matter what you add to the meeting, you'll only make it longer.

Avoid the meeting. The best of all solutions (discussed earlier).

Plan pleasant events following the meeting. Knowing that a Danish and hot coffee are awaiting you right after the meeting will help.

Pray for the end of all unpleasantness in the world. Surely that will include staff meetings.

If there is a serious need for change in your organization, you *can* use the staff meeting to manage management. This should be done sparingly, or everyone will hate you because such a meeting will be a long one. The way to do this is to have an ad hoc committee meeting of people you can trust (surely no more than two or three). Determine beforehand what is needed, garner support from all quarters, and agree to support one another when the issue comes up. Have the most powerful person present raise the issue and support him or her once the motion is on the floor. The Glass House Theory should take over, and you should get your way.

This is a dangerous but sometimes necessary maneuver. Be courageous. And be careful.

Moral:
Staff meeting time is show and tell,
To prove to Ivan all is well.

CAMEL THEORY

**Theory in brief:
A camel is a horse built by
a committee.**

To say that management likes the status quo is to grossly understate the case—they *love* it. From management's viewpoint, the fewer things that change, the better. This is not hard to understand when you realize that many of the existing policies and procedures were developed by those in top management as they rose through the organizational hierarchy.

If you loved the status quo, what would you do? Likely you would devise some way to maintain it. The very best instrument ever devised to maintain the status quo is that old camel-maker, the committee.

Committees move with the speed of a turtle and the thoroughness of a grinding mill. No committee, no legislative body, no group activity of any kind ever produced a drastic

change. That's why management appoints so many committees. They smooth the sharp edges of an idea until it becomes
harmless. Never mind that the idea may have merit.

Like management, a committee is a rudderless ship,
floundering in a sea of indecision. Most of us will serve on a
series of committees throughout our lifetimes, but without in-
struction few of us will ever steer a committee to a safe harbor.
However, it *can* be done. All you have to know is how to become the committee's rudder.

All large committees look alike. And it's a fact that the
larger the committee, the less it will accomplish. Let's take a
look at a typical large committee. It generally has thirteen
personalities. The fourteenth is the "rudder," who, unseen,
steers the committee to its destination. While the thirteen personalities may not all be found on every large committee, the
rudder must be there or the committee goes nowhere.

See how many of these personalities are found on your
committees:

Old-timer chairman. The appointment goes to the one with the
    most seniority, whose store of worthwhile ideas was
    used up long before this assignment. The chairman's
    main job is to let everybody talk and incorporate
    everybody's ideas into the solution. An impossible ap-
    proach—and one of the main reasons why committees
    trying to design horses come up with camels.
Jokester. This guy starts and ends every meeting with a bad
    pun. He doesn't add much to the deliberations, but at

least he breaks up the monotonous conversation from time to time.

Mr. Roberts. This person has read *Robert's Rules of Order*, likes them, and insists that committee meetings be run strictly according to the book.

Official observer. No one has ever heard this person utter a word.

Expert. A veritable fountain of wisdom about things past, this person never has a new idea.

Thinker. This is one of the few committee members who could help solve the problem. But no one ever gives her a chance to say anything.

Politician. Not interested in the progress of the project, this person uses committee meetings to meet new people, renew acquaintances, and promote his or her self-interest.

Discontent. This person feels that all meetings are a waste of time and that this committee is the worst of all. His contribution consists of an occasional burst of profanity.

Note-taker. She believes that everything said is important and writes it down. She will never refer to her notes again after the meeting.

Historian. He knows exactly what you said at the last meeting that you would rather forget. And he won't let you.

Traffic cop. This person knows the committee charter like the back of his hand. He continually tells the committee what it can and can not do.

Unofficial observer. This might be a friend of a committee member or a visiting dignitary. The presence of unofficial observers paralyzes the committee because they are afraid to say anything before a stranger.

Client User. This member desperately needs help from the committee. Needless to say, he is the most frustrated person present.

Let's play fly-on-the-wall at a meeting of Committee B137A at Easy Sales Corp.'s headquarters. The chairman says, "I believe we are ready for a vote on this issue."

MR. ROBERTS: Mr. Chairman, point of order! That request is inappropriate, as there is another motion on the floor.

JOKESTER: It's about time this committee got in motion.

ALL: [Snicker]

POLITICIAN: You could be right, Mr. Chairman, but Mr. Roberts has a point.

HISTORIAN: I recall that we had a similar situation during the third meeting of Committee B13A in 1962. At that time . . . [He gives a five-minute historical sketch of what Committee B13A did.]

THINKER: [Opens mouth to speak . . . and is preempted.]

TRAFFIC COP: I have the charter right here, and I don't think the matter under consideration falls within our scope of authority.

OFFICIAL OBSERVER: [Silence.]

EXPERT: I have an idea. It's a variation of a suggestion adopted by Committee B23F in 1975. [This leads to a

ten-minute dissertation on an unworkable idea that
doesn't apply to the subject at hand.]
DISCONTENT: Horse manure!
JOKESTER: I second Discontent's motion.
NOTE-TAKER: [Busily writes down all comments.]
CLIENT: [Wonders when, if ever, help will be forthcoming.]

"Okay," you say. "I know that committee. I served on
it. What I want to know is, how do you get a committee to
build a horse instead of a camel?"

It's really quite simple. Just practice ruddermanship.
Ruddermanship means you write the committee minutes before the meeting and steer the committee to the desired conclusions. Its kind of like true prophecy—history written in
advance. To do this, just follow the five simple rules listed
here:

Predetermine the length of the meeting. If you need a
long meeting to convince the committee, schedule the meeting
for 9 A.M. If you need to limit discussion to avoid embarrass-
ing questions or senseless discussion, schedule the meeting for
4:30 P.M. on Friday. There are many variations on this theme.

Volunteer for work. Since committee assignments are
usually extracurricular, you will have no trouble landing a key
assignment on the committee. This will give you official clout,
although it may be unspoken.

Be a walking encyclopedia. When you speak, use facts.
If you resort to facts, it will limit discussion. Committees can't
deal with facts.

Force the committee to make a decision. There is only one thing more painful to a committee than voting *for* something, and that's voting *against* it. Make it impossible for the committee to be against your resolution. You can do this by including motherhood, flag, and apple-pie statements. How about this for the preamble to your resolution: "In order to increase profitability and improve Easy Sales Corp.'s sales position, this committee recommends that Harvey Harpooner be appointed to the board of directors." Now, nobody wants Harpooner on the board, but how can you fight against increased profitability and improved sales position?

Be the secretary of the committee. You would be amazed at what a slip of the pen can do to the intent of a resolution. The committee historian, expert, and traffic cop will all insist that the resolution be followed to the letter.

If you do these five simple things, you will become the committee's rudder. In most cases, the judicious use of questions will keep your ruddermanship in the background and make the committee think it is doing exactly what it wants to.

Remember that management forms committees because they feel there is safety in numbers. They figure each committee member will work against the others and, in this way, make sure that no one benefits personally from the deliberations. Committees are *intended* to creep along slowly and masticate everything thoroughly so as not to make a mistake. And it works! Committees seldom make mistakes, because they seldom do anything risky. It can all be summed up in five words: committees maintain the status quo.

However, you *can* steer the committee to profitable waters. And when you do, you will have it your way because the safety-in-numbers philosophy can be used to manage management. How? No manager wants to override a committee. What if the manager should be wrong and the committee right? Anyway, if the committee is wrong, the manager can blame its members. No, it's not likely that the manager will override your committee's well-ruddered decisions.

Therefore, you should think positively about committees. Their weaknesses can be your strengths if you know how to use them. You'll find committees especially useful when you feel the boss might find your personal recommendations suspect. As always, use this theory with caution, but use it— and you will successfully manage management.

Moral:
When to your will the manager won't bend,
A well-steered committee can be your friend.

GROUP
4

Theories for Avoiding Management's Quicksand for Subordinates

---

TOP GRAPE THEORY

OR

Build a Better Rumor and Management Will Beat a Path to Your Door

---

Theory in brief:
The top grape is the unofficial city editor
of the most efficient means of communication
known to man——the company grapevine.

Sam A. Stute and three fellow workers are at the coffee machine for their midmorning break. Sam is the center of attention. As we listen in we hear Sam saying, "Well, it looks like Will Workman's health is going downhill. I'm pretty sure that Kingman is looking for his replacement. Will just can't take the strain of his position anymore."

Now that Sam has the undivided attention of his listeners, he continues: "At first glance, Swann Songue looks like the obvious replacement. After all, he has thirty-one years of service in the company. But his age is against him. Phil Pockets and Randy Rightman would be good choices for the job, but I believe Penny Push will get it."

"Why Penny Push?" ask his listeners in chorus.

"It's simple," explains Sam. "Easy Sales Corp. has not fulfilled its Equal Employment Opportunity quota this year, so that leaves out men. If we had a black employee, maybe Penny would have some competition. But as it is, P.P. has it locked in."

Sam's companions finish their coffee and go off in several directions to spread the news that Penny Push will become the new supervisor to replace Will Workman.

Why do these men have such confidence in Sam? Because he is the oracle of knowledge in Easy Sales Corp. If it has happened, might happen, will happen, or should happen, Sam knows and tells all. Why? Because Sam is the top grape in the company grapevine, a responsible and important position. After all, the company grapevine is the most efficient form of communication known to man. Messages traveling the vine have been clocked at speeds approaching that of light.

While not listed in the *Guinness Book of World Records,* I know of a juicy story that reached each of the 3,687 employees of a company, including the chief executive officer, in less than one hour and eight minutes. And to show the real potential of the grapevine, these employees were located in fifty-two cities in seven countries.

One interesting thing about the grapevine is that it permeates every level of the organization. No one is excluded from the vine's communications, and no one wants to be. No message is too insignificant for the ears of the janitor, the chief executive officer, or those in between.

While there may be many important grapes on the vine, there is only one top grape. An important grape can serve the needs of a small department, committee, or work area, but only the top grape can be the oracle of knowledge for the office, plant, division, or entire organization.

Top grape is not an appointed position. There is no direct compensation for the time spent working at it, nor is there a job description on file for the occupant of this spot. Nevertheless it is a highly coveted, important, and honored position.

The top grape has several important responsibilities:

1—To remember and pass along all gossip, rumors, stories, and even an occasional fact.
2—To be available to talk about the latest happenings at any time, any place, and to anybody.
3—To create useful and believable rumors during slack periods of gossip.
4—To be able to put rumors in historical perspective, thus making them more believable.

To qualify for the position of top grape, one must have:

1—A pleasant voice and colorful vocabulary.
2—Regular access to those in management positions.
3—An overwhelming desire to speculate on what will happen.
4—A reasonable degree of accuracy in the fulfillment of

rumors passed (access to confidential information through the boss's secretary will substantially improve the batting average).

5—Bionic eyes (including the ability to read upside down while talking to people at their desks).

6—The capability to enrich rumors and fill in missing tidbits of data.

7—The appearance of wide-eyed righteousness and honesty.

The top grape is a powerful tool through which to manage management. But subordinates in progressive organizations must watch carefully to be sure that unscrupulous management are not using the top grape as a double agent.

This devious management ploy uses the top grape in a variation of the Trial Balloon Theory, a reverse twist called dropping an anchor. Whereas in the Trial Balloon Theory subordinates send up trial balloons for management's reactions, in the anchor variation management drops an anchor to see if it "catches" the fancy of their subordinates.

The anchor rumor is leaked to the top grape, who then passes management's message to the right people. As the story passes from ear to ear, it will be modified according to the conscious or unconscious desires of the grapes, big or little, ripe or green.

When the rumor returns to management, the similarity of the returned rumor to the original message is directly proportionate to the acceptance of the idea by the subordinates.

Now let's return to the rumor about who will get Will Workman's job.

The fact is that the rumor did not originate with Sam A. Stute. Penny Push used the Top Grape Theory to obtain the position she wanted. She knew that Will Workman was a trustworthy, hard-working employee. She also knew that he had a health problem. Oh, it wasn't too serious, but he had lost twenty-three working days during the past year. This information was readily available from Wendy Watch, the company spy.

Penny passed rumor number one to Sam. This was the story about Will's health worsening and that he might have to retire because of it. When Sam passed on this tidbit, it alerted management to the "fact" that they might have a position to fill.

Knowing there were others more qualified for Will's job than she, Penny again tapped the top grape. This time she passed on the word, again from Wendy Watch, that the company had not filled its Equal Opportunity Employment quota this year. This put her in line for the job, since there were no blacks available.

What made Penny's rumors really work was the top grape. Sam performed magnificently for Penny when, on the basis of two rumors, he speculated that Penny would get Will's job. This got management to thinking about the logic behind the rumors. For that reason, and due to the pressure put on them by the top grape, management selected Penny Push for the supervisory position when Will "decided" to retire.

Penny's intelligent use of the Top Grape Theory worked for her. It will work for you too.

A final illustration will show the usefulness of the top grape in getting decisions made in a timely manner.

Let's assume that a bad snowstorm occurs and within an hour Easy Sales Corporation's parking lot is blanketed with six·inches of snow. The top grape sees trouble ahead. Traffic will be hopelessly snarled by five o'clock, and the workers may become involved in accidents that could result in time lost from the job.

As usual, management is not managing. Ivan Kingman looks out the window, but he sees no problem. He lives close to headquarters.

Something must be done. Sam, our trusty top grape, springs into action. He passes the rumor that the office and plant will close at 3 P.M. due to the blizzard. This is the fastest-moving type of grapevine communication, since it has a limited life span. Penny's type of rumor can be savored over many days or weeks. But not this weather rumor. It has to reach all levels of the organization in time for a decision to be made well before 3 P.M.

A quick-spreading rumor such as a plant or office closing causes great excitement. The switchboard lights up like a Christmas tree as supervisors from outlying areas check out the authenticity of the rumor. The switchboard operator has to call the boss's secretary, who in turn asks the boss about the truth of the rumor. If enough people call, Kingman will succumb to the pressure and make a *decision*—something he is very unaccustomed to doing.

An actual 3 P.M. closing scores yet another point for the top grape and adds to his prestige and credibility. With continued success, the top grape and those who use him wisely will come to have more to do with running the organization than many high-level managers—and that's not all bad.

Moral:
If you want to tell the truth
or simply spread a rumor.
Tell it to the topmost grape;
He'll reach your prime consumer.

WE GOTCHA
THEORY

Theory in brief:
Benefit plans, like chains, are designed
to keep you in one place.

If you love freedom, you've got to watch those benefit plans. They are used to lure you into the organization and to keep you from leaving. If you stay with the company long enough to let your benefit plans mature, you have been lured into the company trap and the door has been slammed shut on you. The organization knows it's gotcha, and you know it's gotcha. From that moment on, you can either be in big trouble, or be as happy as a lark, depending on whether you really like your job.

Once you know the We Gotcha Theory, you begin to

wonder who benefits from the benefits. A fringe is defined as a decoration. Okay! How often does someone decorate something they don't own? Are you decorated with company fringes? If so, then the company probably owns you.

We ought to examine the benefit plan closely, because not all benefits are obvious. The number-one benefit the company holds out is comfort and security. Many of us are just like our managers. We hate change. We want to be comfortable in our old clothes, at our old desks, our old chairs—and in our old jobs. If we feel comfortable and secure, we are likely to remain with the company—even if we dislike our jobs. The second fringe benefit that the company offers us is permanency, friends, and familiarity. The very thought of packing up and leaving can outweigh many personal dislikes.

There is another major category of fringe benefits quite familiar to us. These are vacations, hospitalization, life insurance, pension plans, sickness benefits, paid holidays, sick leave, company stores, company picnics, sports leagues, and so on. All of these can be measured in dollars and cents—as our bosses have pointed out many times. And, as is the case with the other benefits, the longer we stay with the organization the more valuable they become.

As we grow older, the value of our benefit packages increases as our saleability to other organizations decreases. Equal opportunity notwithstanding, most companies believe the myth that people over forty are not desirable employees. The fact is that managers believe anyone over forty who can break the We Gotcha Theory is not dependable or trustworthy. Such people are usually looking for work they enjoy, and what manager wants an employee like that?

There are three paths of progression within any organization.

First, there is the path represented by a rather flat curve, starting anywhere on the salary/authority scale and remaining virtually the same with just a slight increase during an entire career. This path belongs to those with serious personality problems. Such people cannot cope with the business world and its machinations or with the theories in this book.

Second, there is the path following a steady but shallow rise after starting at a given point on the salary/authority scale. This is the path of the average employee who understands a few of the theories in this book but applies them haphazardly. If they work at it, they can rise far above average in both authority and salary.

Third, there are the meteoric astronauts of the organization whose paths of progression can be plotted as a steep rise to the top of the authority/salary scale. These employees are extremely ambitious and are willing to give everything for "success" as they see it. These persons apply every theory in every way possible with special emphasis on the Company Photograph.

The company generally scales your pay increases to your age. Raises come most rapidly in the younger years, and less rapidly in the declining years. Why? Management tries to provide for your material needs so that you won't be tempted to leave the organization until your fringe benefits mature. Then they've gotcha!

Management has another ploy that works toward your staying with the company: increasing benefits over time. The longer you stay with the company, the less likely you are to leave. When you become eligible for five weeks vacation, are you going to take a job offering one week? If you have become eligible for thirty days sick leave a year, will you take a job offering nine? What if your pension benefits are 50 percent vested? Suppose you have become entitled to life insurance equal to three times your annual salary? You'll think twice before leaving if you have all this. Your company won't divulge the statistics, but it's obvious that 95 percent of those who stay with an organization for five years retire from that organization. And that's what your company is counting on. They've gotcha!

How can you escape from the We Gotcha Theory? Only by determination and good planning. If you stop to think about it, you may find that the very benefit plans that hold you to the organization can help you leave. You may find the equity you have built up in your retirement fund can become your freedom fund. Suppose you have built up one year's salary or more in the retirement fund. Pack up the family and move where you've always wanted to live. While you're at it, get a job you like. That's freedom now!

One way to find out if your organization's gotcha is to take a piece of paper and draw a line down the middle of it. On one side list the things you want out of life and your job. On the other side of the page, list your current lifestyle and job conditions.

Here's a typical list:

What I Want	What I Have
I would like to travel.	I never leave home or office.
I would like a warm climate.	It is cold half the year here.
I would like to be my own boss.	I am an abject slave.
I wish I could be more creative.	I do repetitive jobs all the time.
I want enough money to live well.	I make enough money to live well.
I want a nice home.	I have a nice home.

If your list looks like this, then you are a candidate for a freedom fund. However, if you make the list you may find you have just about what you want. If so, use the theories in this book to improve your situation. But don't let your company say, "We Gotcha!" Find out what you want and take steps to get it. And remember the cry—freedom now!

Moral:
If the company's gotcha, but the job's no fun,
Make a break for freedom, find your place in the sun.

DON'T WISH FOR A
NEW KING
THEORY

Theory in brief:
Don't wish for a new king, the old one
is bad enough.

Your troubles are not unique. All subordinates have problems with superiors. It's been that way since the beginning of recorded history. The system may be bad, but it cannot be changed. So do yourself a favor. Don't wish for a new king, the old one is bad enough.

Let's start at the beginning. When you were born, God provided you with superiors called parents. They are a motley group but you can't change the system. Under their tutelage, you grew, matured, and finally broke away. In the home, this is called "cutting the apron strings."

It's the same in business. When you are assigned to a department, you have superiors. We call them "managers" (although this is misleading). When you start a new job, you are like an infant. You must crawl before you walk, and walk before you run. So you do what the boss says the way he says to do it. We understand our position relative to the manager.

However, just as with children, we grow, mature, and, hopefully, break away into a higher position in the organization. And, as children eventually learn Mom and Dad are not infallible, comes the day when we find the manager doesn't know everything. To you, as a new employee, this probably came as a shock. You thought, "If the boss got his position knowing so little, maybe the other managers did too." This shakes your confidence in the organization. And with good reason.

Back to the home scene. In our teens, we began to rebel against our parents' rules and regulations. Insubordination turned into open rebellion and we did as we wished. During this series of skirmishes and, at times, open warfare, we often wished for new parents. Through divorce and being placed in foster homes, many young people find new parents. They are often worse than the first set.

Businesses run on the same basic system. Only there's very little love in business. But isn't it true that, after we are on the job for a time, we feel we know how to do things better than the boss? We attempt to change methods and procedures. We often wish for a new king.

How many times have you wished for a change and, when you got it, didn't like it? You ran away from home so you could be king, only to find the nights cold and candy bars unfulfilling. Or you hoped that one of your teachers would get a transfer, and when she did, the new teacher was worse than the old. You divorced your spouse and married a louse.

Never wish for a new king, the old one is bad enough!

"But I am miserable," you protest. "I want a new king!" Wrong. If you stop to think about it, you'll realize that contrary to the old saying, you *can* teach an old king new tricks. Perhaps an example of life in Easy Sales Corp. will help prove the point.

Dee Endd was extremely unhappy with her boss Peter Pinch, the controller. Peter Pinch kept pushing Dee to perform. Every time Peter went on a trip, she found herself anxiously looking through the paper for news that his plane had gone down. Worst of all, she was disappointed when it hadn't. When he returned, Dee would sigh, "If only he would leave Easy Sales Corp., my life would be better."

One day Dee's wish came true. For some unknown reason Peter left the company. Harvey Harpooner got the nod. As Dee's new boss, Harpooner came down hard on her. "I can't believe it," cried Dee, "my new boss is much worse than old Peter Pinch!" Dee's life was miserable before Harpooner arrived on the scene, but he made it much worse. The new king Dee had wished for fired her just eighteen days after he took Pinch's place.

Have you learned your lesson, Dee?

Don't wish for a new king, the old one is bad enough.

The boss is the king. Whether it's in the mailroom, the steno pool, a particular department or division, the supervisor or boss is the king. Kings do not have to be logical. Kings do not have to be practical or smart. The king is the boss. In countries that still have monarchs, the new king will be the eldest child of the present king. He or she will look like daddy. Ever notice how *all* monarchs look and act alike? See the king wave to the crowd. Kings like crowds. See the king sign the bill into law with a flourish. Kings like flourishes. See the king strut at all major events of the nation. Kings like to strut at all major events of nations.

Kings are born to be what they become. It's the same with corporate kings. Have you ever noticed that heads of secretarial pools look alike? Have you noticed that corporate controllers always write with sharp pencils and speak with sharp tongues? Aren't salesmen always smiling, telling jokes, and full of bs? Did you ever see a happy guard? Aren't receptionists carbon copies of one another?

Do people seek positions? Not really. The position seeks the person. If someone becomes a corporate controller, it's because he or she is corporate controller material. Therefore, if you wish for a new corporate controller, you will always get a corporate controller type. Don't expect anything else. Sam Smoothwater is destined for the sales department. Harvey Harpooner is a natural-born controller. And a Mary Mouth will always head the clerical group. You might think that when Mary Mouth leaves, pleasant Wendy Watch will get the job. It's not likely. For every Mary Mouth you send out to pasture, there are two more applying for her job.

Of course, there are rare exceptions. But they never happen by chance. They must be maneuvered by using a combination of several theories in this book.

Your job, then, is not to wish for a new king but to properly train the old one. If you are to train him or her effectively, there are several things you should not assume:

—Never assume your manager knows how to manage.
—Never assume your manager understands your job.
—Never assume your manager knows how to solve problems or handle situations.
—Never assume your manager will look out for your best interests.

It would seem that the training department is in charge of training. Not so when it comes to your boss. As a subordinate, you are responsible for your king's training. Don't take a chance on a new king. Mold the present one into the type of king he ought to be.

There are several reasons why new kings are worse than old kings. When you get a new king, you automatically revert back to the parent-baby relationship. You don't know what the new king expects of you, so you must crawl before you walk, and walk before you run. How long did it take to get the old king to listen to you? Years, right? Do you want to go through that again? The new king might never listen to you. He might even lop off your head! Remember Dee Endd?

No matter how miserable your present king is, you have established some mutually agreed-upon ground rules. If you are a late sleeper, your boss has learned to live with that even though he may dislike it. If you loathe working overtime on Fridays, your king has come to accept it. With a new king, you start at ground zero. Nothing is taken for granted. Everything must be worked out from scratch.

Now you know why you shouldn't wish for a new king. But you should make the old one into the king of your choice. If the boss makes a mistake, tactfully show him how it could have been avoided. If the boss doesn't understand, explain to him. If something out of the ordinary is about to happen, prepare the boss. Kings don't like surprises. Whatever the old king's weaknesses, help him improve. In time, you'll make him into a tolerable king—and that's about the best you can hope for.

And when the boss does well, don't forget to say "Good boss."

Moral:
If you think your king is bad,
Train him not to be a cad.

GOFOR THEORY

Theory in brief:
The way to get a job done is to have
someone else do it.

A gopher in this context is not a cute little animal with buck teeth. It's another name for a subordinate—and we spell it GOFOR. Management loves the feeling of power they get by ordering subordinates to gofor this and gofor that. And sooner or later, every subordinate must recognize that their gofor assignments should get top priority.

From the time we were infants, the Gofor Theory was ingrained in us. Our parents made us gofor the newspaper, gofor something from the refrigerator, and gofor groceries at the supermarket. In school, we became gofors of the teachers. These were happy gofor assignments. Take this to the office. Run this note down to Mrs. Jones in Room 411. We cherished each gofor assignment given to us.

Nowadays the gofor is an automatic, remote-control switch. We can change channels without moving, our garage door opens upon our arrival, our homes are air conditioned by gofor thermostats. But these robot gofors will never replace the human kind.

Secretaries have been called gofors since the forties. Ivan Kingman's secretary was so proud of the designation, she wore a T-shirt to the company picnic with the word gofor emblazoned across the front in bright red letters. Ivan laughed, as did the others, for they all knew it was true. The fact is, however, virtually everyone is a gofor, not just secretaries.

Take Will Workman for example. He was working overtime, double time, any time to meet a critical deadline. Ivan Kingman had made it clear to Will that he *would* finish the report on time or update his resume. Will is making every minute count. While Will is engrossed in his project, Ivan storms in the door with an urgent request.

"Will, a friend of mine just called and wants my opinion of an article on zero-base budgeting," says Ivan. "Would you get me a copy of the magazine?" That's gofor number one. "And Walt, get Denny Dart's and Phil Pockets's opinions on the subject." That's gofors two and three. On his way out the door, Ivan says over his shoulder, "Oh, by the way, pull all the information together and get back to me with it as soon as possible." That's gofor number four.

How should Will react? If he understands the Gofor Theory, he will drop his top priority project and take care of Ivan's requests. If not, Will may wait until he finishes his project to respond to Ivan's requests. At evaluation time, Will will wish he had sprung into action and gotten that information on Ivan's desk within thirty minutes. When the big boss asks you to gofor something, it immediately assumes the top priority, whether it seems important to you or not.

Why do managers assign gofor tasks to their subordinates? Generally it's because they just don't want to gofor those things themselves. Could Ivan have found the magazine himself? Of course, but he just didn't want to. Could he have called Denny and Phil to get their opinions? Yes. But again he didn't want to. That doesn't make it any less important to follow through quickly and efficiently on the assignment. Remember your boss may not always be right, but he is still boss.

Now that we have gofors in proper perspective, how can we use them to our own advantage? To do so, we need a few more basic facts. They are:

—We are all gofors for our superiors.
—All our subordinates are our gofors.
—Gofor assignments have the utmost priority.
—We should never refuse a gofor assignment.

If we understand these four simple truths, we are ready to use the Gofor Theory to our advantage. By advantage, we mean getting as many "brownie points" from each gofor assignment as possible while doing very few gofors personally. To achieve this feat, let's formulate our gofor implementation plan. Here are the steps in the process:

Make a list of those whose gofor you are. Always accept gofors from these people.

Make a list of people who are your gofors. Give gofors only to these persons.

Anticipate and volunteer for gofors before they are assigned to you. Example: if you and your boss are eating lunch together and you know it will be paid for by the company, volunteer to put the bill on your expense account. If you are in a meeting and it appears it will run through coffee time, volunteer to get coffee for the group.

Reassign as many gofor assignments as possible. This is acceptable as long as you follow through to make sure your boss gets what he wants when he wants it. In the gofor chain of command, the buck stops at the bottom gofor.

Bosses like good gofors. If the time comes when the manager must choose between a competent worker and a competent gofor, he will choose the gofor every time. Competent workers take care of inanimate organizations. Competent gofors take care of the personal wants and whims of managers. You should never underestimate the importance of gofor assignments in your own career development. And don't resent them. Remember, the vice president of your organization is the president's gofor. And the president is the chairman of the board's gofor.

In fact, that's probably how they got where they are today.

Moral:
When the boss speaks, don't dare be a loafer.
It pays to be his personal gofor.

"OH, BY THE WAY . . ." THEORY

Theory in brief:
Unpleasant news is often delivered after a casual
"Oh, by the way . . ." when you least expect it.

"Oh, by the way . . ." ranks right in there with "Beware the Ides of March" when it comes to bad news. It's a phrase used to ease into bad news such as being fired, being told of your deficiencies, the removal of your favorite unauthorized status symbol, or the addition of a zinger to contracts and projects.

Contrary to popular opinion, managers hate to deliver bad news. They have been known to delay discharging an inept employee for three years because they dread delivering the bad news. The fact is that one of the joys of being a manager is being able to give raises, promotions, status symbols, and special favors. To avoid as much unhappiness as possible, managers use the "Oh, by the way . . ." ploy to blurt out the bad news, then make a fast getaway.

To work well, the "Oh, by the way . . ." must be used when it is least expected. Let's see how management uses the theory, and then we'll see how you can use it to manage management.

Scene 1

Penny Push is rushing down the hall to the restroom. A moment of desperate need. Penny's supervisor grabs her arm just as she reaches the restroom door and says, "Oh, by the way, Penny, we won't be able to give you a raise this year because our profit picture is bad." Penny can't stop to talk about it at this moment and doesn't find her boss for three days. Her supervisor is an expert "Oh, by the way . . ." user.

Scene 2

Will Workman is reviewing his latest report with his boss. The boss compliments Will on the fine work he has done and comments on how pleased he is to have a willing worker like him on the staff. Will is feeling great. He thanks his boss for the kind words and heads for the door. "Oh, by the way," calls the boss, "we have a special assignment for you at our storage depot just north of Fairbanks, Alaska. We'd like you to leave Sunday afternoon. Here are the details of the assignment. Study them over tonight and tomorrow." A stunned Will accepts the papers and, when he opens his mouth to comment, he notices that the boss is on the phone with his back to him. At this precise moment Wendy Watch, the boss's secretary, ushers in the next visitor. Will has no choice but to leave and prepare for his new assignment.

Scene 3

At five minutes to five on a Friday payday, Harvey Harpooner drops by Swann Songue's office for a chat. After four minutes of sports and weather, Harvey says, on his way out the door, "Oh, by the way, Swann, we've got to cut back on the number of employees. I'm very sorry, but this will be your last day. "Of course," he hastens to add, "we'll give you a month's severance pay, the accrued balance in your pension account, and a good reference." Since Harvey has a dinner engagement, he apologizes for having to run and exits, leaving Swann Songue dazed and confused. Nice move, Harvey.

While all these examples seem cruel and cowardly (and they are), few subordinates have any idea of the agony the boss goes through before, during, and after giving out bad news. Some will go to any length to avoid being the bearer of gloom. They delegate the task to subordinates, send memos, or have the board pass a resolution. Others drop hints with ominous phrases like "Looks like we may have to cut back on the number of personnel units in this department." All such statements are clues that an "Oh, by the way . . ." is on the way.

History has shown that the best defense is a good offense. This is no less true with an "Oh, by the way . . ."

How can you avoid the business end of an "Oh, by the way . . ."? One of the best ways is to join the boss's team.

Offer to help the boss to perform his most onerous task, dispensing bad news. If you are giving an "Oh, by the way . . ." you can't be receiving one.

Let's relive those three scenes and see what could have been done to avoid being zapped by "Oh, by the way . . ."

Scene 1

Penny Push should know that profits are down for the year. She should also know that she is not the apple of her boss's eye this year. Knowing these facts, Penny should go on the offensive. Okay, Penny, do your stuff. Well before it's time for raises to be given, go see the boss and use the Glass House and Double-Cut theories. Ask for a big raise. You'll be cut to a small raise, but you'll probably get a raise of some kind. Remember, Penny, attack, attack!

Scene 2

Will Workman should keep in touch with the company grapevine. Top grape Sam A. Stute knows and tells all. Will hears that someone is going to be tapped for that north-of-Fairbanks-Alaska assignment. Will knows one thing: he's the Florida type. "So," reasons Will, "I'll help the boss out. Who could we send to that storage depot in the frozen north? Phil Pockets, that's who. He'll do a great job, and this will get Phil a promotion." So Will explains to the boss why Phil would be just the right person for the job. And even offers to lay the "Oh, by the way . . ." on Phil for the boss. That is an offer no cowardly boss can refuse. Enjoy Florida, Will!

Scene 3

Swann Songue knows times are tough. He has been around long enough to know that in such times someone is likely to be laid off. Okay, Swann, get busy. Stuff your problems down the rathole, work both ends of the clock, on every occasion possible tell Ivan Kingman he's right, use every theory in this book that might help raise your status—and do it now!

There are many uses of the "Oh, by the way . . ." and, by the way, none of them bodes well for you. They always give the appearance of a casual afterthought, but they are always well planned. Some of the characters in the Easy Sales Corp. cast are masters in the exotic uses of "Oh, by the way . . ." Here are some examples:

Mary Mouth (*office gossip*). Mary makes a lot of visits to everybody's office. She engages in excessive conversation which generally terminates with "Oh, by the way . . ." It generally assaults someone's honesty, integrity, or loyalty to you or the company. For example, after discussing generalities for a while, she says, "Oh, by the way, did you hear that computer services' last printout had an error every third line?" Now it's your turn to give her more grist for the gossip mill. Don't do it. She'll use it against you. And one thing is certain: the knife will be in your back as soon as she gets to computer services.

Sam A. Stute (*top grape*). Sam knows how to make things happen by starting rumors and passing them along the grapevine. His "Oh, by the way . . ." is designed to get information or make some rumored event a reality. He'll say something like, "Oh, by the way, did you hear that the factory and office are closing at three o'clock on account of snow?" Your call to Ivan Kingman's secretary may trigger a question to Ivan, a look out the window, and the closing of the factory and office. Denny's a pro!

Wendy Watch (typical subordinate). Many subordinates use "Oh, by the way . . ." to lay bad news on the boss. After placing letters on Mr. Harpooner's desk at five minutes to closing, Wendy says, on the way out the door, "Oh, by the way, Mr. Harpooner, I'm pregnant." If she says, "Oh, by the way, *Harvey,* I'm pregnant," this might have even greater significance.

Keep in mind the myriad possibilities of "Oh, by the way . . ." It has awesome power. If you know one is coming, you can devise an offense against it. But if it catches you by surprise at just the right time, you have had it. If your manager does you in with a well-directed "Oh, by the way . . ." read this chapter again. You may be able to avoid the next one.

Moral:
If you're always prepared for an "Oh, by the way . . ."
On the company's roster you'll probably stay.

Harem Theory

Theory in brief:
It's hard to say no to a good-looking girl.

Sexism rears its ugly head when managers hire certain levels of personnel. Many managers cannot rise above their prejudices when faced with the need to decide between hiring a competent person or a beautiful person. You may be mentally rebelling at that statement because it presupposes that beautiful people are not competent people. Logic may seem to be on your side, but, unfortunately, beautiful people are often hired to do jobs they are not equipped to handle simply because they look so good. The result? Incompetency.

Besides, many managers pride themselves on the physical beauty of their staffs. This is particularly true of female employees. Industrial psychologists explain why this is so: most work is dull, and the sight of a pretty girl brightens up an otherwise drab and boring day. And think of the conversation beautiful women generate. The fantasies that the male employees conjure up overshadow the latest rumor from the company grapevine, the Superbowl, and that day's political intrigue.

Before telling you how to use the Harem Theory to manage management, let's review the five general personnel selection criteria in use today. While managers may select different criteria at different times, a given manager will generally concentrate on one of the five. You may not like what you hear, but these five criteria are used every day by managers around the world.

> —Hire the most competent person to do the job. (Very rare!)
> —Hire the best-looking person who applies.
> —Hire females based on their breast size.
> —Hire the best-dressed applicant.
> —Hire a member of a minority group. (Imagine how quickly a pretty, well-dressed, big-breasted member of a minority would be hired!)

Now you may be thinking, "That's detestable. There is absolutely no reason to hire beautiful people over average or ugly ones." Wrong! There are quite a number of uses for beautiful people on the staff, as any sexist manager will tell you. For example:

> —To give the boss bad news. Kings seldom slay gorgeous messengers.

—To ask someone to do a job by 5 P.M. Friday when it's already 4:45.

—To sit in on meetings in order to distract dissenters or to cheer up attendees when the news is gloomy.

—To greet visitors and put them at ease before business meetings.

—To serve as the centerpiece for departmental photographs.

—To serve as a fringe benefit for management and visiting dignitaries.

Notice that none of these uses involves productive work or doing a particular job. Of course, some beautiful people are hired for a job which they just happen to be able to perform. But all too often, this is not the case.

As a subordinate, you must recognize the fact that managers like harems. The reason is that a beautiful harem is a status symbol. Other managers, clients, and visitors from the home office will openly admire the harem—and the manager who surrounds himself with it.

There are at least two reasons to keep in mind the Harem Theory. First, if you are part of the harem, your potential for advancement is limited: you are probably working at a job you cannot perform well merely because your boss likes to look at you. *Ipso facto* he won't move you up, and you are probably (or will be soon) very frustrated. Second, you can use the Harem Theory to manage management. But how?

Denny Dart can tell us. Of all the employees at Easy Sales Corp., he understands the Harem Theory best. When

Denny came to work for Harvey Harpooner the average age of the accounting department staff was 52.5, with an average of just over twenty years of service. This was a competent staff. They did their jobs well and, except for backstabbing and gossiping, Harpooner was satisfied with their work.

But Denny knew human nature. He knew that something was needed to get Harvey in a better frame of mind. By a stroke of pure genius, Denny got grumpy, troublesome Mary Mouth a lateral promotion. Through a series of deft maneuvers, using several theories in this book, Denny got Harpooner to appoint pretty Wendy Watch to Mary's position.

The fact that Wendy was not too swift in accounting matters did not worry Harpooner too much. He liked to watch Wendy. So he compensated for her lack of expertise by cracking the whip a little harder on the other members of the accouting department staff to take up the slack. Wendy soon became number one in Harvey's harem.

How did Denny benefit from managing Harvey Harpooner and establishing his harem for him? First, Harvey's attitude improved. And his colleagues gained a new respect for his managerial abilities. For Denny, this meant that Harvey was not looking over his shoulder as much as before. And more important, Harvey was very grateful to Denny for brightening up his life. This meant that Harvey always seemed to owe Denny a favor. And Denny knew how to make the most of Harvey's indebtedness.

Since Harvey was now better respected by top management, he was most likely destined to move up the hierarchical ladder. Denny had a close eye on that and intended to move with Harvey.

To benefit from the existence of harems, you must observe the unwritten but universally accepted "do's" and "don'ts" of harem usage. You never learned these at business school, but they are as important to your career as anything you learned in the classroom.

Harem Do's

—Openly admire the boss's excellent hiring skills.

—Help the boss to add attractive bodies to his harem.

—Honor the queen of the harem (undue demands on her can be your undoing).

—Make the queen and her entourage the subject of discussion at coffee breaks, luncheons, and other gatherings.

—Bestow favors on the queen and her court (your boss will love you for them).

Harem Don'ts

—Don't become socially involved with members of the harem during office hours (and only clandestinely after office hours).

—Don't marry a member of the harem (unless one or both of you are willing to be expelled from the organization).

—Don't become responsible for the removal of a favored member of the harem for such superfluous reasons as efficiency or economy.

—Don't pinch, fondle, or touch any member of the harem without the express approval of the sultan (in other words, forget it).

If you understand the importance of the harem to your boss, you can advance your cause by doing the do's and refraining from the don'ts. This is one of the few theories which can bring you benefits by mere inaction. Those who do the don'ts will miss out on a promotion or find themselves missing altogether, depending on the manager.

So keep in mind the Harem Theory. It's one more tool to help you manage management.

Moral:
Managers love to fulfill their duties
Amidst a flock of beautiful cuties.

FOSSILIZATION
THEORY

Theory in brief:
A fossilized person is one who has joined
the ranks of the active retired.

A scientific definition of a fossil is the remains of animal life from some previous age. A business definition of a fossil is a person with outmoded and fixed ideas. When a person becomes a fossil, his or her creative capabilities are gone. A fossilized brain is like a tape recording, the only words and music you can get from it is what's already on it. No matter what song you want to hear, it will only play the same old tune.

People fossilize at any age. And, for them, it's synonymous with retirement. The only difference is fossils remain on the payroll. Some organizations describe their fossils as the "active retired" or, to use the trade jargon "ineffective plateauees." One of the youngest fossils in history was Dee Endd who joined the ranks of the active retired when she was twenty-seven. She is now forty-seven and still working (we use the term loosely) for Easy Sales Corp.

Let's examine Dee Endd's business career to see how and why she fossilized. In the beginning, Dee had everything going for her. She graduated *magna cum laude* from a major Ivy League business school. The recruiter from Easy Sales Corp. wooed her with glamorous stories of life in the business world. The offer was irresistible. The salary was good, the fringe package was good, and the opportunity for advancement appeared good. So Dee enthusiastically accepted a position as a management trainee at Easy Sales Corp.

When Dee started work there, she was twenty-two. Over the next three years, she spent two months in eighteen different departments. Thirty-six months of "keep-busy work" had not completely discouraged her, but it was taking its toll.

Dee lived in anticipation of her first big assignment. The day came and she read the organizational directive with excitement. There it was! Dee Endd was made assistant to the administrative assistant of the assistant section head of the auxiliary mail room. Wow!

During her orientation sessions, Dee learned the importance of getting to work on time (Both Ends of the Clock Theory), keeping detailed records of everything (Alibi File Theory), performing the little jobs for the boss (Gofor Theory), learning who in her department knew what was going on in the company (Top Grape Theory), as well as showing up on time for the weekly staff meeting (Show and Tell Theory).

As Dee looked over her work station (Potted Plant Theory) and contemplated her committee assignments (Camel Theory), she began to have serious doubts about her future with Easy Sales Corp. The next month she argued against Ivan Kingman's latest nonsensical policy (You're Right Ivan Theory), lost a confrontation with Tom Tough (Walking Encyclopedia Theory), found her latest ideas had been stolen by Denny Dart (Calendar Theory), and was left holding the bag on a disastrous project because Phil Pockets had escaped responsibility (the Houdini Theory).

A nervous wreck, Dee took some time off (Mental Health Theory), but was still in no condition to work when she returned. She hung around Easy Sales Corp. for about five years (We Gotcha Theory), until management finally let her speak at meetings (Blue Mold Theory). By now, Dee had reached her fossilization point. She became a fossil on her twenty-seventh birthday and has been considered a model employee ever since. She hasn't been accused of doing anything wrong, and no wonder—she hasn't done anything at all. She is one of Easy Sales Corp.'s "active retired."

If you want to succeed in business, you must avoid fossilization for two reasons. First, you may not want to become a zombie at twenty-seven. Second, you may want to avoid becoming a fossil long enough to gain management's respect so you can inherit some fossils to work for you. Are they worth having? In some ways, yes. Fossils cause no problems. They never stab you in the back. They don't want your job or credit for what you do. On the other hand, they aren't going to contribute much creatively. What you need to learn is how to recognize fossils and use them.

How can you recognize fossils? By their blind adherence to company policies and procedures. Fossils wear them like badges of honor. Any deviation from the policy manual would require a fossil to accept authority, which is out of the question. Fossils, like their companies, are content. They act like a puppy after a full meal, all curled up asleep by the fireplace.

If you want fossil production, give them repetitive routine tasks. They do such jobs well. If you want the policy manual, bylaws, or performance manual revised or coded, a fossil is the person for the job. They also do well in positions requiring an accurate knowledge of company policy. Just don't ask them to do anything creative or innovative. It isn't in them.

What motivates fossils? Their major enjoyment in life is telling other employeees and customers what *cannot be done* because it is against company policy. Given such a job, they will be content until actual retirement twenty years hence.

Are there many fossils out there in businessland? There are indeed! About seven of every ten employees over thirty years of age are fossilized to some degree. One psychologist said that the average person has no more than five original, creative ideas in a lifetime. You should try to get five ideas from all your colleagues before they fossilize.

Now you know how to keep from becoming a fossil. You aren't one, you know, or you wouldn't be reading this book. But keep checking. If you find signs of fossilization, take steps to stop the trend. If necessary, kick off the traces and infuse new life into the old you. If they haven't gotcha, there's still time to change jobs and find a challenge. Whatever you do, don't become an old fossil!

Moral:
If you fossilize, my friend,
Your career is at its end.

SPINNING PLATE
THEORY

Theory in brief:
You can keep only so many plates spinning before you or
the plates break. But management doesn't know this.

You remember that old vaudeville act where the performer kept a large number of plates spinning high in the air on thin sticks. It looked as though there was no limit to the number of plates he could keep spinning. But the performer knew his limit and worked accordingly.

Every day in the business world, subordinates are forced to perform the spinning plate act. But the difference is that the manager refuses to admit that subordinates are limited to any given number of plates. So the managers keep stacking them up on their performers.

The typical manager sees that Will Workman has six

plates spinning. Since they are all going pretty well, he adds a seventh . . . then an eighth . . . and so on until the subordinate pleads "No more plates" or one falls to the ground and shatters. If one falls, the manager will assume that Will is incompetent. If the subordinate cries "No more plates," the manager may put the plate on somebody else's stack.

The plates take various forms: units sold, dollar volume, units of work, projects, and so forth. For example, if you sell 100 cars this year, you may be asked to sell 110 next year. So eventually you will miss the quota and the plate will come crashing to the floor. At times, managers go berserk and throw a whole stack of plates on the pile. This might increase the salesman's quota from 100 to 140 cars in just one year. In the business world, this is referred to as "dumping" on employees.

If you are in production, your next plate could be five units per day of increased production. This is added to the plates you already have spinning. If you accept the plate, you had better get it spinning and keep it spinning or you will be labeled incompetent.

Whatever your job, the quota will be gradually increased until management finds your breaking point. As a subordinate, you must realize what is happening and be prepared to yell "No more plates" in a way that will convince but not alienate management. Not of least importance is your timing.

How can you tell your boss "No more plates" without getting clobbered? One thing you must do is almost let a plate or two fall to the floor. Just before they fall, you get them going again. As your boss watches you "save the day" time after time, he may come to the conclusion that you have all the plates you can handle.

Several theories in this book will provide you with other ways of shouting "No more plates" inoffensively. Let's review some of them:

Trial Balloon Theory. You could send up the idea of giving the new plate to someone else, or the idea of giving an already spinning plate to another subordinate when you accept the new one. Another trial balloon might be the statement "I don't know if I can keep any more plates spinning." If your boss seems agreeable to any of these or other trial balloons, make a concrete suggestion.

Man on the Moon Theory. This requires you to accept any number of plates, but request plenty of help to spin them.

Alibi File Theory. Since you know that sooner or later a plate will drop, build a complete file ahead of time so you can blame somebody else.

Houdini Theory. Brag to the boss about how many plates you can keep spinning, accept an inordinate number, then escape by turning them all over to another person while they are still spinning.

Rathole Theory. Sweep the broken pieces down the rathole, and ask for new plates.

Moral:
If spinning plates have you berserk,
Pick a theory and go to work.

YOU'RE RIGHT, IVAN THEORY

Theory in brief:
Your boss may be wrong, but
your boss is still boss.

Managers are generally insecure. That's why they look to their subordinates to bolster their egos. These managerial security blankets are commonly referred to as "yes men" or, in the language of the liberated, "yes persons."

A yes person is supposed to provide aid and comfort to the boss on demand. A typical request for comfort is the question "Isn't that right, subordinate?" The correct response is "You're right, Ivan!"

While many managers proclaim that they dislike yes persons, they secretly dread all confrontations with subordinates. What the manager really wants is to be right all the time and have his subordinates agree on his rightness. Managers will stoutly maintain that they want brilliant, ambitious subordinates—but they hire and promote those who agree with them.

In effect, the manager is really saying that subordinates who agree with him are brilliant and ambitious. Unfortunately, all of us have this tendency. For instance, how many of your friends and close associates go around telling you "You're wrong, friend." Apparently, it is human nature to surround ourselves with yes persons.

Properly saying "You're right, Ivan" is not a simple art. You can learn a lot through trial and error, but perhaps I can help you avoid that hard teacher, experience, by discussing how to say "You're right" in various situations. You must carefully study the boss's question if you are to give him the "You're right" he wants. Let's see how Sam Smoothwater handles several situations:

Situation A

Ivan Kingman and Sam are examining sales reports for the past year. Ivan says, "Sam, sales are down in District A. I think we should change sales managers, don't you agree?" Sam knows there is only one answer to that question: "You're right, Ivan."

Situation B

Same review of sales activity. This time Ivan says, "Sales are down in District A. Looks like it's time for a change of sales managers. What do you think, Sam?" Sam knows that Ivan wants a change but has a slight doubt in his mind. He wants subordinate reinforcement. Sam responds, "You should change sales managers, Ivan, because all the other sales districts have shown increases."

Situation C

Same situation, but Ivan's comment has a new twist. "Sales are down in District A," Ivan says. "Looks like we have a problem. What do you think, Sam?" Sam is in a spot. He is not sure what Ivan thinks the problem is. Unless he finds out, he could blow it. The first thing Sam should do is use the thirteen-second-delay technique. Bosses generally cannot wait thirteen seconds to speak, so it's pretty certain that as Sam "thinks" about his reply for this brief period, Ivan will come up with the answer to his problem by saying something like, "Yep, it's about time to change managers." If so, Sam can use the reply in Situation B. However, should Sam opt not to use the thirteen-second delay, his answer should be "You're right, Ivan, we have a sales problem." This safe reply will give Ivan the chance to tell Sam what the solution is.

Situation D

Here we have the same situation, but Ivan says, "Sam, we have a sales problem in District A. Would you analyze the situation and come back later today with a recommendation?" In this case, Ivan is fishing for a solution to his problem. The easiest way for Sam to come up with the right answer is to use the Trial Balloon Theory at once. A comment by Sam such as "Looks like we might have to replace the sales manager" will get some kind of response from Ivan. For example, Ivan might say, "That's what I've been thinking." With this information,

Sam can write the conclusion to his report first and work backward to support it. His report and recommendation will say "You're right, Ivan."

Situation E

The same situation, but Sam is put on the spot when Ivan says, "Sales are down in District A. Harvey Harpooner tells me we should replace the sales manager. What do you think, Sam?" Sam is treading on thin ice because Ivan hasn't tipped his hand as to whether he agrees with Harpooner. In this case, Sam can put the Company Photograph Theory to work. He remembers the latest Easy Sales Newsletter, in which there was a photo of Harvey and Ivan smiling with Ivan's arm around Harvey's shoulders. "You know, Ivan, I think Harvey's right," Sam says—and Ivan smiles. Sam isn't named Smoothwater for nothing. If Sam's quick analysis had turned up evidence that Harvey Harpooner was not one of Ivan's boys, Sam would have opted for the opposite answer.

Situation F

Same situation again, but this time Ivan says, "Sales are down in District A. My initial reaction is to get a new sales manager. What's your opinion, Sam?" This is another example of managerial insecurity. It's really a managerial trial balloon. In this case, Sam can feel free to give Ivan his frank opinion because Ivan is really looking for help. This time your opinion will be right, Sam.

Obviously, your responses to your boss's questions must be sensitively attuned to subtle differences in wording. Too, you must know his mood and carefully assess his tone of voice. Like all managers, he will transmit enough information for you to come up with the right response. It's possible to say "You're right, Ivan" every time by properly phrasing it.

Remember that the boss may not be right, but the boss is boss. Disagreements over unimportant issues or those already decided by the boss are worse than useless—they are detrimental to your personal advancement.

The only time it is acceptable to say "You're wrong, Ivan" is when it affects you personally. If Ivan says to you, "I'm going to give you a five percent raise this year, is that okay?" you know that Ivan would like to hear you say "You're right, Ivan" but he will allow you to disagree without falling into disfavor. Ivan may or may not give you a bigger raise, but he will think "There's a person with guts," and that can't hurt you.

If you choose to say "You're wrong, Ivan" when he has already made up his mind, you are fighting a losing battle. And even if you win the battle, you will most likely lose the war. When your manager asks you a question, think about its ramifications. If it's not vital for you to take a stand on the issue, say "You're right, Ivan."

Moral:
If you would rise to the very top,
Say "You're right, Ivan" and never stop.

GROUP
5

Theories to Make Life at Work Easier for Yourself in Spite of Management

---

POTTED PLANT
THEORY

Theory in brief:
There's more to life than money and power.
There are status symbols.

How do you know if you have made it? You can tell by your status symbols if not by your income. The big boss, Ivan Kingman, knows who's in charge when he pulls into his underground parking space next to the elevator. Controller Harvey Harpooner knows his niche in the hierarchy when he enters his top-floor, corner office overlooking the center of town. Penny Push *loves* her white telephone with three incoming lines. And, I admit, my ambition in life was to get a potted palm in my office and have the company gardener water it every morning.

Every organization has its own status symbols. The

higher you go, the snazzier the rewards. Remember how you used to judge people's wealth when you were a kid? The kid whose mother bought him a Good Humor bar every day was just a notch above everyone else. The first kid on the block to get a new bike was looked up to by one and all. Ten-speed bikes were ritzier than five-speeds. The ones who bought their lunch at school were better than those who brown-bagged it. And so it went.

When we grew up and moved into the business world, we found things hadn't changed much. Important people have underground parking spaces near elevators. Important people have offices with a view. Important people have telephones with multiple lines. And, yes, important people (like me!) have potted plants in their office.

Unimportant people don't have these things. Unimportant people do not even have telephones. Unimportant people lay their coats on a chair instead of hanging them in a clothes closet. Unimportant people have grey desks and only one guest chair without arms—or none at all!

In the cold, cruel world of business, you can tell important people from unimportant people not by what they do but by their status symbols or lack of them. Easy Sales Corp. has a person to decide who gets what status symbol—Mary Mouth. As head of the office services department, she knows precisely what is and isn't permitted in anyone's office. She has a book showing how to furnish the offices of all five pay grades. And she will fight to the death anyone who tries to break the status code.

Mary has the awesome responsibility of making sure

there are no status symbol violations. She can be seen making the rounds regularly, checking to see who's been naughty or nice. Mary's hawk eye can spot a violation three offices away. Take the case of Ken Census, for example.

When Ken was in Pay Grade No. 3, he was not allowed to put pictures on the wall. But Ken was overcome by the bicentennial celebration. He bought a picture of the American flag and put it on the wall in back of his desk. It wasn't long before Mary spotted this out-and-out status symbol violation. But Mary couldn't bring herself to make Ken take down a picture of the American flag. After all, hadn't she always wanted to be a Marine infantryman?

Clearly this had to be an executive decision. Mary talked to Tom Tough. But Tom had been a Marine. Harvey Harpooner finally settled the matter by authorizing Mary to put out a memorandum saying,

Memo To: All Easy Sales Corp. Employees
From: Mary Mouth, office services manager
Subject: Condition of Offices

Now hear this. Ivan Kingman, president, has instructed me to get the offices looking professional. Therefore, you will observe the following rules:

1. Display no personal mementos on your desk.
2. Do not display pictures of people you like, including family members.
3. Do not thumbtack or scotchtape anything to the walls such as calendars, maps, jokes, pictures, or *anything else.*

4. Remove all unauthorized plants from offices.
5. Remove all unauthorized pictures from office walls.
6. Use only equipment purchased and authorized by the company.

If these rules are not complied with by the fifteenth of the month, violators will answer directly to the president. Remember this is all for your benefit.

Cordially,
Mary Mouth

While the whole status symbol system can be a constant source of irritation, it pays to understand the importance management attaches to it. Suppose you didn't understand the Potted Plant Theory. Your boss might offer you a status symbol you thought was silly and you would therefore reject it. Silly or not, accept status symbols. It raises you a notch in the organizational hierarchy. Realizing this, you might even request a status symbol to improve your position in the organization—but your timing must be right.

On the other hand, knowledge of the Potted Plant Theory will help avoid desecrating status symbols by criticizing the system or failing to admire the boss's corner office, his underground parking space by the elevator, even his potted palm. Your boss may not make much more than you do, but he does have his status symbols. Take those away and what does he have?

The unfortunate fact is that if you can talk your boss or top management into the idea that you should have more and better status symbols, you will command more respect and admiration from your colleagues when you get them. So use the Potted Plant theory to advance your career. The Negative-Positive and other theories in this book will help you get the status symbols you want.

Moral:
Status symbols may strike you as funny,
But the truth is, they're worth more than money.

DOUBLE DESK
THEORY

**Theory in brief:
If you have two work stations, you're
free to do your job.**

Management—whether parents, teachers, or employers—tries hard to keep us in one place. It's your duty to spend time legitimizing your being in more than one location. That's where the Double Desk Theory comes in. Here's the theory: If you have only one work station, one room, or one desk, you are expected to be there all the time. On the other hand, having two desks, two work stations, or two rooms, frees you to move around without complaint from the boss. It is to your advantage to have freedom of movement. It is to management's advantage to restrict your movement. Let's see what it's like with only one desk.

When you were young, your parents would say, "Go to your room!" They wanted to know where you were. Your teachers would say, "Sit down at your desk." They knew where you were. The boss says, "Be at your desk promptly at 8:30." He wants to know where you are. You explained to your mother, "I'm over at Ann's house." She said, "You're supposed to be at home." You told your teacher, "I'm going to the library." She said, "Don't leave this room." You explained to the boss, "I have to stop at Ace Office Supplies on the way in." He said, "Order it by phone." How can you establish your right to be away from your primary work station? By using the Double Desk Theory.

Some people have likened the employee with one work station to an animal in a zoo. The boss is the zoo keeper and you are the animal in the cage. Any time the boss wants to see you he rattles your cage. Then there's the guided tour through the zoo. When Wendy took Norman New on his meet-the-guys tour of the offices, she could count on seeing all the subordinates in their cages. She could say, "That's Will Workman; see Will work." Or, "This is Dee Endd's desk. Hi, Dee. Isn't Dee neat?" Life with one work station has definite disadvantages. For instance, you don't dare arrive at work five minutes late even though you've got double pneumonia. Why? The boss checks your work station.

Until you get your second desk, here's a tip that will help you get a little freedom. If you're going to be late, be very late, and if you are going to leave early, leave very early. Being five minutes late or leaving five minutes early gives the appearance of disorganization and lack of interest in your job. However, if you leave for home in the middle of the day or call in sick for half a day, it looks legitimate.

You may not remember it, but early in life you established your right to move around even though management assigned you only one desk. One second desk we all learned to use was the bathroom. No one can stop you from leaving your work station to go to the toilet. And in school, where did you go when you needed a mental health break? To your second desk in the nurse's office, the guidance office, or the library. At work, you have places that correspond to these second desks: the coffee machine, the cafeteria, the supply room, the Xerox machine, the water cooler, and—this is a biggee—*other peoples' work stations.*

Phil Pockets uses the Double Desk Theory. How did he work it out? Phil was in charge of Easy Sales Corp.'s stockroom. This was his primary desk. However, Phil had to make several trips to the warehouse each day. By using several theories in this book, Phil convinced his boss that he needed another desk at the warehouse. Although he liked to keep his subordinates in one cage, Harvey Harpooner reluctantly agreed to Phil's request. Sometimes working conditions can force management into giving you a second desk.

Let's call Phil's primary work station Desk A and the warehouse station Desk B. Now that Phil had Desk B, Harpooner assumed Phil was working there if he was not at Desk A. Phil no longer had to worry if he was a little late in the morning. If he got to Desk A an hour after opening time, his boss figured he had been at Desk B. In fact, Desk B was great therapy for Phil (see Mental Health Theory). Of course, some people go too far. Phil worked the ultimate Double Desk ploy. He renamed his boat from "Phil's Pholly" to "Desk B." Then

Phil could go fishing and tell the people in the stockroom, "I won't be back this afternoon, I'll be at Desk B."

Done properly, the Double Desk Theory gives you enough freedom of movement to get your job done without being hassled by management. When you have only one desk, you worry constantly about being late in the morning even though you worked until midnight the night before. You worry about getting back late from lunch even though you left late because of business commitments. And you worry about losing your job if you take five minutes to do an errand on Friday that will take you three hours on Saturday.

If you have a second desk, the boss can't hound you every seven minutes about the status of the job on which you are working. If you have a second desk, your boss can't waste your time discussing every minute detail of your latest project. You are freed from all problems except how to do a job accurately and on time. Management doesn't know it, but left alone their subordinates will work longer and better. Since they won't leave you alone, break out of the zoo by getting your second desk.

The Double Desk Theory means freedom now. If you have only one work station, start to establish your right to a second. You'll be doing yourself and management a favor.

Moral:
The Double Desk will get you far:
The boss will not know where you are.

DEEP SIX
THEORY

**Theory in brief:
Don't do the job you don't
have to do.**

Harry Truman had a famous sign on his desk. It said simply: THE BUCK STOPS HERE. This meant that there was no one higher up to whom to pass the decision. Subordinates understand Truman's motto to mean that sooner or later somebody has to perform. While it's true certain important decisions get passed up the line until someone finally has to act, most work is passed down from subordinate to subordinate until someone looks around and finds there is no one else to pass the job to.

So it is the subordinates at the bottom of the heap who end up doing all the work. Middle-level managers fulfill most of their duties through creative delegation. If the whole world could delegate, nothing would get done. Take heart, you at the low end of the totem pole!

Former President Nixon popularized the Deep Six Theory on some tapes he later wished he had deep-sixed. When asked what to do about certain documents or data, Nixon would say, "[Expletive deleted] Deep-six it." That meant get it out of sight, way out of sight! The objective of deep-sixing is to be sure that the document, data, or what-have-you is never heard from again.

How does this theory help the overworked? If you know which assignments to deep-six, you can handle assignments without ever working on them. Confused? Let's see how Will Workman discovered the secret of deep-sixing.

Will is burning the midnight oil at Easy Sales Corp. Tom Tough can delegate faster than Will can work, so Will has to work sixty or seventy hours a week. As Tom receives assignments from Harvey Harpooner, he writes a note and clips it to the assignment. The message is cryptic: "Will, please handle." In Tom's mind the assignment is complete, since he has obeyed Harvey Harpooner's cryptic note which said: "Tom, handle."

Some attachments to assignments carry as many as seven "——, please handle." Of course, six are scratched out and the poor soul who is seventh has to do the work.

After one of these heavy work sessions, Will Workman left the office perspiring and caught pneumonia. Don't feel sorry for Will; it was the best thing that ever happened to him. At the time he contracted pneumonia, Will had seventeen jobs in his in basket with notes from Tom saying "Will, please handle."

Will returned to work two weeks later. Had Tom done any of Will's jobs? Not on Will's life! As a welcome-back gift, Tom had put fifteen new assignments in Will's basket.

Will was under strict orders from the doctor, who forbade him to work more than eight hours a day. In sheer desperation, Will put the seventeen old assignments in his top desk drawer and began working on the fifteen new ones. Will worried about the seventeen assignments in his desk drawer until his ulcer flared up. A week went by and Tom Tough said nothing about those seventeen assignments. Another week went by. At the start of the third week, Tom asked about one of the seventeen assignments. Will dug it out, completed it, and went on with the current batch of assignments.

After four weeks back at work, no one had even mentioned the other sixteen assignments in Will's drawer. Will's birthday was on the eve of the fifth week. As a birthday present to himself, he deep-sixed the sixteen assignments by tossing them into the wastebasket. It is now two years, three months, and seven days later. No one has ever asked Will about those sixteen assignments.

Ever since his birthday, Will writes the date on each assignment when it is received. If at the end of four weeks no one has asked about the assignment, Will deep-sixes it. Will spends his evenings at home with his wife and kids, his ulcer has disappeared, and his nerves are steady.

A devious device, you say? Unfair to Will's company? A poor work attitude? Perhaps not. First, let's find out how essential the assignments were. Of course, a manager would never deep-six an assignment. But, remember, managers almost never have to complete an assignment personally. They delegate. So, how essential were the sixteen assignments Will deep-sixed?

One of Will's assignments came into existence during a leisurely lunch Ivan Kingman was having with Harvey Harpooner. Ivan casually mentioned seeing Wendy Watch walking through the lunchroom with a huge stack of filing. "I wonder how much it costs us to store all that paper?" Ivan mused. It was just an idle question that flashed through Ivan's mind. But Harpooner wondered whether this was Ivan's subtle way of questioning his approving three filing cabinets that Denny Dart had requisitioned the previous day.

As soon as he got back from lunch, Harpooner sent Tom Tough a memo in which he expressed his concern about the cost of filing Easy Sales Corp.'s paper work and specifically asked how many files were filled with nonessential documents. Tom looked over the memo. He hastily scribbled on a memo sheet "Will, please handle."

Tom felt that Harvey Harpooner might also be concerned about how long certain documents were being stored. He passed a memo on to Mary Mouth asking her to check it out. Mary stapled a note on Tom's memo saying "Will, please handle." That was two of the sixteen.

Neither Tom nor Mary was really concerned about this information. They were just fulfilling their duties as middle managers by delegating responsibility. If Ivan or Harvey ever asked about paper storage, they were covered. They would say, "Will is working on that," and promptly tell Will to get on the ball.

Was Will wrong to deep-six these two complex but meaningless assignments? Had he spent the time to obtain this meaningless information, would he have been productive? Did he do a disservice to his company?

Here are five simple steps to help you to a happier, healthier, more successful life in your organization.

1—If you receive an assignment you must do, do it.

2—If you receive an assignment you want to do, do it.

3—If you receive an assignment you don't want to do, delegate it.

4—If you receive an assignment of dubious value, date it and file it.

5—If no one asks about a dubious assignment for four weeks, deep-six it.

Moral:
When jobs by the gobs are given to you,
Deep-six'em by dozens, and you'll be through!

INSIDE THE GATE
THEORY

Theory in brief:
Don't ever get hurt unless you're
on company property.

Legally, companies consider employees to be two entities: the employee at work, and the employee not at work. Most benefits cover the employee while at work. A few benefits cover the employee when not working, such as group health insurance, life insurance, and, in some cases, salary continuation plans.

However, while an employee is at work the benefits increase dramatically. They include full medical coverage, special life insurance policies up to several hundred thousand dollars, salary continuation for the rest of your life, as well as state and federal employee compensation policies.

That's why you should get hurt only at work!

When are you at work? That may seem like a simple question, but it's not. Legally you are considered to be at work if you are on the premises of your employer; or, when off premises, if you are conducting business for your employer. For example, if your boss asks you to go to the store to buy something for Easy Sales Corp., you are considered to be at work from the time you leave until you return. If you get into an accident, fall, or get hurt in any other way, you are covered just as fully as though you were at your work station. It's the same on a business trip. You're covered until you get back.

If you return to your work station at night, whether paid or not, you are considered to be at work as a bonafide employee. Even if you are hurt while participating in company-sponsored activities such as softball, basketball, or the like, you are covered as an employee at work. You need to know this if you are going to use the Inside the Gate Theory.

Denny Dart understands this theory. And he clearly understands the difference between an employee at work and an employee not at work. Denny has given his wife and children specific instructions on what to do if he is hurt while not at work.

"If I am injured in any part of the world," Denny explained, "come get my body immediately, by the fastest way possible. Spare no expense. Then take my body, alive or dead, and return it to the property of Easy Sales Corp." Denny's exact words were: "Throw my body over the gate any time of the day or night. Once I am safely inside the gate, our future will be secure."

Phil Pockets is another employee who knows his way

around the fringes of the benefit package. One night he was installing a pool table in his basement when a heavy slate fell on his foot, badly mangling it. His wife, Pick, headed for the phone to call an ambulance. Phil called out urgently, "Don't call the ambulance. Help me into the car." In great agony, Phil got in and was driven at high speed to Easy Sales Corp.'s property. Although it was late Sunday night, Phil had a passkey. He unlocked the door and his wife dragged him to his office. Then she walked home, leaving the car by the gate. Phil was content. He was safely inside the gate and would be considered an employee at work. It took Phil thirty-seven months to recover—but he got full pay in addition to a large settlement. And, because of his "employee-at-work" injury, he is assured of an easy job the rest of his life. After all, what company would fire an employee hurt in the line of duty?

Of course, if you want to use the Inside the Gate Theory, you'd better do some advance planning. Where are the guards located? When do they make their rounds? These are basic questions because if a guard spots someone throwing their spouse over the fence, it might arouse his suspicion. What about signing the attendance log? Denny foresaw this problem and had his wife sign it with the same signature she used to cash his checks.

Now you're probably saying that the Inside the Gate Theory is immoral. With that kind of conscience, you'll never benefit from the theory. People like Denny and Phil argue that it is immoral for your boss to fire you after you get hurt away from the job. If he is an equal opportunity employer, why does he fire you for being crippled? "And another thing,"

Denny would say, "suppose you leave work so frustrated from management's aggravation that you smash your car and yourself to pieces on the way home. Who is really at fault—you or your employer? And if you hurt yourself painting your house in the dark because you are tired from working overtime the last five nights, who is responsible for your injury?"

You are the only one who can decide whether the Inside the Gate Theory is for you. One thing is certain, getting hurt on company property is not all bad.

Moral:
If hurt off work, instruct your mate
To throw your body over the gate.

MENTAL HEALTH
THEORY

Theory in brief:
You can't work if you're
a basket case.

You say your boss is on your back, you have two weeks' work
to do by next Thursday, and more just landed on your desk.
You say your arch rival got the job you've been counting on,
your raise wasn't big enough to cover the rise in cost of living,
and the boss just announced an austerity program. You say
your boss gave you five more assignments like the one you
asked him never to give you again, you've got to work overtime on your anniversary, and your training assignment in
Hawaii has just been cancelled. Yep, you've got, or are well
on your way to getting, a mental health problem.

What are the symptoms of mental health problems? The most common are churning stomach, migraine headache, acute aggravation, inability to think clearly, fits of anger, and nausea. Among the more advanced symptoms are alcoholism, chain smoking, deteriorating relations with the spouse and kids, dog kicking, and bleeding ulcers.

Who said heart disease was the number-one killer in the United States? It's really management!

Why is everyone concentrating on improving physical health when it's mental health that's tearing us up? Take Will Workman for example. Due to extreme frustration on the job, he has smashed fourteen fenders in four years; six by running into cars and telephone poles in the company parking lot, five trying to force his way into traffic leaving the parking lot, and the other three when Will kicked his fender to vent the anger built up during a week of frustrations at Easy Sales Corp.

In the business world, it's survival of the fittest! To be successful, you must learn how to keep mentally healthy. Alcohol, tobacco, and drugs may provide short-term relief, but they will kill you in the end. What you need are survival techniques without bad side effects. Let's examine some methods used by people who have managed to remain sane while gainfully employed:

Use your sick leave. While some may frown on this, the fact is that, when you have blown your mind, you are sick. Since personnel departments are singularly unenlightened in the area of mental health, they accept such excuses as virus, diarrhea, female problems, psoriasis, and, perhaps, severe ache of the lower colon. Keep track on your calendar which excuse you last used.

Use your annual leave. While this is going to the extreme, there are times it is the only way out.

Leave your work station. How long you leave depends on the gravity of your mental health problem. If it's minor, just walk to the water fountain. If more serious, consider a visit to the employee's lounge or a walk outside around the building. If extremely serious, use your sick leave.

Get some physical exercise. A few moments or a lunch period of vigorous activity will get your blood circulating and infuse your entire mind and body with life-giving oxygen. Although not as satisfying, this is a good substitute for punching the boss in the nose. The latter path is best if you're calling it quits anyway.

Gorge your stomach. Just get up from your desk, walk to the nearest vending machine, and buy the most sinfully fattening candy bar you can find. Have pie à la mode for lunch. Buy a whole pizza. Or partake of some other long-desired treat. This is sound psychology: the guilt feelings you get from gorging will wipe out the frustration you experienced at work.

Send out some résumés. It doesn't matter if you aren't really planning to leave. The idea that you just might find a better job will immediately improve your mental health. The thought that one month from today you may be able to tell off the boss and walk out the door will do wonders for your outlook on life.

Go on strike. Just stop working. But don't picket. No one has to know but you. Furthermore, it's probably beneficial for your company to stop work when your mind is messed up because it may take longer to undo the mistakes you make than it will to do the entire job when your mental health improves. During work stoppages you can daydream, plan vacations, work out your home budget, or just sit there and glare.

Pray for help. If your best efforts can't solve the problem, then seek guidance from above. God wants us all to be happy.

Only by keeping a positive mental attitude can you be happy and successful. So don't let the company break your spirit. Use these mental health methods freely. By doing so, you will avoid ulcers, smashed fenders, alcoholism, and other problems. Remember no one can harm your mental health unless you let them. So don't let them!

Moral:
If your mind is nearly wrecked,
Try a trick they won't expect.

OH GOD THEORY

Theory in brief:
In business you should practice what you preach,
but never *preach what you practice*.

On Monday morning you would think Easy Sales Corp. the most religious outfit in the world. If you walked up and down its hallowed corridors, you would see all the employees with their heads in their hands saying, "Oh God!" That's about the extent of religious practice in most businesses.

In the big corporations, management believes religion to be a threat. They feel that serving God will distract you from your main job, serving Easy Sales Corp. Ivan Kingman, who represents all top managers, says on behalf of his firm, "I am your company, and you are my employees. Thou shalt have no boss besides me." Many corporations demand the utmost loyalty and consider you in some way unfaithful if you have strong religious convictions.

The Oh God Theory says that if your boss catches you being religious, he will make you pay for it one way or the other. The theory insists that the chief executive officer plays God to the employees. That's one reason this book was written. To help get you out from under his godlike thumb.

God created the heavens and the earth and made man to multiply, fill the earth, and subdue it. God created life and wrote the rules of the game. God's rules are called Commandments. Ivan Kingman created Easy Sales Corporation and hired all the employees. Ivan created the business and wrote the rules of the game. He calls these rules corporate policies and procedures. We call them the ten commandments:

I—Thou shalt have no other boss beside me.

II—Thou shalt not bow down to any graven image (except the company logo).

III—Thou shalt not take the name of Easy Sales Corp. in vain.

IV—Remember the Sabbath, to keep it wholly for overtime.

V—Honor thy manager and thy mother.

VI—Thou shalt not kill time.

VII—Thou shalt not commit adultery with the boss's harem.

VIII—Thou shalt not steal from Easy Sales Corp.

IX—Thou shalt not bear false (or true) witness against Easy Sales Corp.

X—Thou shalt not covet thy fellow worker's goods (you've got your own benefits).

As with God, so with Ivan Kingman. If you break one of his commandments, you are in trouble. And forget those commandments Moses got, for, if you obey those, it means disobeying Ivan's.

Business has evolved a set of informal policies and procedures regarding religious practice. You won't find them engraved on tablets of stone, but they are just as permanent. There are no-no and yes-yes rules.

NO-NO RULES

—Don't display religious objects such as a Bible at your work station.

—Don't pray for guidance with your eyes shut (even if you are sleeping or meditating, your boss will still think you are a religious fanatic).

—Don't openly discuss religion (sports, weather, and the latest company rumors are okay).

—Don't be a member of a minority religious group (if you are you'll pay for it).

YES-YES RULES

—Do support accepted community projects such as the annual charity drive.

—Do be kind to the sick, needy, and bereaved but only within your organization.

—Do unto others before they do unto you.

These are the rules from the company's standpoint. The fact is you *can* practice your good religious principles in business but don't let anyone know that's what you're doing. Ken Census has done this for years. He is kind, thoughtful, and fair. And people love him for it. Randy Rightman is a lot like Ken. The difference is that Randy tells people he is practicing the Golden Rule. He says, "See Randy. See how good Randy is. Randy is kind. Randy is sweet. See what a holy man Randy is." People resent Randy.

Ken's religious philosophy can be summed up in this story about his son. Ken got home from work one night and his son greeted him as he got out of the car: "Daddy, Daddy, see how good I can hit the ball." With that, Ken, Jr. threw the ball up in the air and swung the bat with all his might. Strike one. He threw the ball up again and swung even harder this time. Strike two. "I'll get this one," said Ken, Jr., tossing the ball up and taking the mightiest swing yet. Strike three.

The boy was dejected and tears came to his eyes. Big Ken consoled his son with words of wisdom: "Never mind, you're a great pitcher."

If you learn anything from the Oh God Theory it should be this. Let Ivan *think* whatever he wants to. Just don't let him become your God. If you use the theories in this book, he'll keep on thinking he is supreme but you'll be maneuvering him to your good and the company's benefit.

Moral:
Some companies demand of you,
The worship that God is due.

HOUDINI THEORY

Theory in brief:
Projects are great to start but watch out for
the end. It might be yours!

Who's Houdini, you say? Just the greatest escape artist of all times, that's all. Harry Houdini could escape from ropes, handcuffs, straightjackets, and boxes that had been nailed shut. Houdini claimed no supernatural powers. He attributed his ability to perform mind-bending feats to physical conditioning and common sense. One thing Houdini always did was prepare adequately.

There are many modern-day Houdinis in the business world who make the original look like an amateur. Unlike Houdini, today's corporate escape artists shun publicity. They make their escapes look like accidents, forms of punishment, or great personal sacrifices. Nevertheless, they are master es-

267

cape artists. At Easy Sales Corp., Denny Dart is *the* master of escape. Denny starts a lot of projects, but at their finish he is invisible—if they fail.

For this reason, Denny will try anything. He's at it again. Here he is approaching Harvey Harpooner with what Denny says is the greatest thing since sliced bread. According to Denny, he can devise an inventory control system so sensitive to market conditions that even the coffee in Harpooner's thirty-cup percolator will run out exactly at quitting time each night. "The savings will be stupendous," declared Denny.

Harpooner had no reason to doubt Denny. After all, it was Denny who saved so much money by putting hot-air dryers in the restrooms in place of expensive paper towels. It was Denny who suggested having the company Christmas party on Saturday so Easy Sales Corp. could wring an extra hour's work out of every employee. And it was that same Denny Dart who revealed that if the cafeteria chairs were hard and uncomfortable, people wouldn't sit in them so long.

Having reviewed all of Denny's past triumphs, Harpooner thought, "No more wasted coffee!" His enthusiasm was undisguised when he told Denny, "Go to it!" As Denny walked away from Harpooner's office he recalled the words of a fifty-seven-year-old athlete who rowed a twelve-foot boat across the Pacific Ocean: "There are two good parts of a project—when it starts and when it ends."

The long-distance rower was right. In between the beginning and the end of a project there is nothing but a lot of hard rowing. The photographers and press see you off and see you land, but in between it's out of sight, out of mind, except for the occasional question, "Are you still rowing?" Years of experience had convinced Denny that he had to escape the rowing phase of his clever projects.

Now that Project Inventory System was approved, Denny maneuvered Will Workman into the project as second in command. This level of authority entitles Will to work out and implement the details. In other words, Will is doing the rowing. While it may appear that both Denny and Will are now handcuffed inside a nailed up box, that's not the way it really is.

Denny, like Houdini, began working his way to freedom as soon as the nails were in the top of the box. Meanwhile, Will is working to get the job done. Denny already has the handcuffs off because he is planning to blame Will for anything that goes wrong. After all, isn't Will the one who worked out the details? And that's not all.

Denny has plans to get his side of the box opened by somebody on the outside. How will he do that? Before the project ends, Denny will use one or more ploys to have the entire project placed on Will's shoulders. And Will won't be able to blame Denny either.

Here's what Denny might do:

New assignment ploy. Denny arranges to get pulled off the inventory control project to fill some special need. Denny still gets credit for the project if it succeeds because he suggested it.

Promote from within ploy. Denny explains to Harvey Harpooner that since Will has really been the driving force behind the project, he should get the credit for it. "This," beneficently explains Denny, "would give Will the recognition he deserves and the added responsibility will be good training."

Poor patient ploy. If all else fails, Denny will have his appendix out. It's a relatively harmless operation (the surgeon says) and, regardless, anything's better than being blamed for a project that has bombed. By getting the operation at a critical point in the project, Denny assures the appointment of a new leader.

Projects are like automobile races. The contenders make their move during the last few laps. As they near the last lap, they jockey for position so that they can get across that finish line first. But there is one difference: when you are working on a project, you do not want to cross the finish line first if the project is a failure. The reason is simple. On a project failure, the first one across the finish line gets not the checkered flag, but the guillotine.

That's why you need your own series of counter-ploys to outwit the Houdinis in your company. Then, when you work on a project, you will be alert to what Denny is doing, and you can drive some new nails into the top of the box on his side when he thinks he is escaping. Here are three counter-ploys that work:

Naïveté ploy. When the big boss, Ivan Kingman, is about to lay his sword on your shoulder to make you Knight of the Shining Inventory Project, naïvely say, "I really am not best qualified for such an important project, but Denny would be great for the job." (If the project can't lose, graciously accept Knighthood.)

George Washington ploy. When Harpooner tries to put you in charge of the project (at Denny's insistence), say, "I cannot tell a lie. Denny deserves all the credit. It just wouldn't be right for someone else to lead his project."

Poor patient ploy. At some critical stage of the project, have your appendix out.

Use these ploys to defend yourself. If Denny dreams the impossible dream, make sure the boss knows it was Denny's dream and have Denny tell him so. Don't wake up in Denny's bed when the dream ends.

Moral:
When the project you don't start,
Keep awake and play it smart.

THE LESSON

OR

If Someone Doesn't Point the Ship in the Right Direction, It Will Run Aground

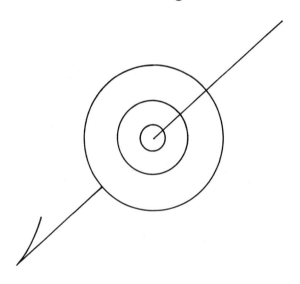

Drucker, Maslow, and Hertzberg—all giants in the field of management theory—have written volumes for the modern manager. Their principal message concerns how managers can get more work out of their subordinates through proper motivation. At the same time these concepts were being fostered, other giants were exposing organizations and their managers for what they really are, namely:

Murphy—who professed that what can go wrong will, and at the worst possible moment.

Parkinson—who said work will expand to fill the available time.

Peter—who proved that managers will rise to their level of incompetency.

Macoby—who recognized the "gamesman" executive who uses business for fun.

Perry—who proclaimed that management, like gravity, is a holding force with the primary function of keeping ideas from rising to acceptance.

These two ideologies of organization and management are not conflicting. Both have as their objective doing the best job possible with the least possible resources. The difference is that Drucker, Maslow, and Hertzberg believe in top–down management. The only trouble with that theory is it doesn't harmonize with the facts. Today, organizations are run from the bottom up or they stand still.

The theories you have just read are meant to help you, the harried subordinate, get things done with the minimal amount of resources and the maximum amount of personal satisfaction and recognition. The deviousness of some of the theories is not what recommends them. They are recommended because they work. They seem devious because you must make them work without management's realizing it or they will thwart your efforts.

THE LESSON

We hope that the message of this book will be incorporated into the Ten Commandments* of Success:

1—Work hard, for hard work is the best investment anyone can make.

2—Study hard, for knowledge enables you to work more intelligently and effectively.

3—Use your initiative, for ruts deepen into graves.

4—Love your work, for then you will find pleasure in mastering it.

5—Be precise, for slipshod methods result in shoddy work.

6—Be spirited, for then you will successfully overcome difficulties.

7—Be yourself, for personality is to a man or woman what perfume is to a flower.

8—Help others, for true greatness is attained by giving opportunity to your fellow man.

9—Love people, for unless you feel right toward your fellow man, you can never be a successful leader.

10—In all things do your best, for if you have done your best, you have done everything. If you have done less than your best, you have done nothing.

*Paraphrased from Charles Schwab's famous ten commandments.